12/08
13.95

Conventions Today

Brian Senior

Better Bridge Now

CHESS & BRIDGE LTD

First published in Great Britain in 2001
by Chess & Bridge Limited
369 Euston Road, London NW1 3AR

Distribution:

USA and Canada: Master Point Press
331 Douglas Avenue, Toronto, Ontario, Canada M5M 1H2;
tel: (416) 781 0351; web: www.masterpointpress.com

For all other enquiries, please contact the publishers,
Chess & Bridge Limited, 369 Euston Road, London NW1 3AR;
tel: 020 7388 2404; fax: 020-7388 2407;
email: chesscentre@easynet.co.uk; web: bridgemagazine.co.uk

British Library Cataloguing in Publication Data.
A CIP record of this book is available on request from the British Library.

ISBN 0-9530218-2-3

Typeset by
Wakewing Ltd, 73 Totteridge Lane, High Wycombe, Bucks HP13 7QA

Printed in Great Britain by
The Cromwell Press, Trowbridge

Foreword

There are millions of bridge players all over the world, but the vast majority of them have never read a single book on the subject!

However, if you have the desire to increase your knowledge and improve, then your watchwords should be 'read and play'.

The *Better Bridge Now* series provides you with the perfect opportunity to develop your bridge skills, by covering all the essential elements of the game.

No matter what system you employ, conventions will play a part. It was therefore an obvious choice for the *Better Bridge Now* series to include a title on the subject.

Brian Senior has long been recognised as one of the world's best player/writers, and in this book he breaks new ground by not only describing the most important conventions in modern use, but also by suggesting which will pay dividends.

This book will not only help you to decide what to incorporate into your partnership's armoury, but also help you to understand the many weapons that might be used against you at the table by your opponents. It may even inspire you to create a convention of your own!

Thanks must go to the American Contract Bridge League for providing many of the photographs.

If by some chance you don't find your favourite convention in this book, please let us know! You can email the London Bridge Centre at bridgeshop@easynet.co.uk

Mark Horton
Editor
Better Bridge Now

Contents

Introduction

The aim of this book is not to list every convention in current use. Were I to try to do so, the list would run comfortably into four figures and you could use this volume as an aid to body-building. Rather, my intention is to include only the best and (not necessarily the same thing) most popular conventions in any given area of bidding. You might say that these are the conventions that a social or club player might find useful and a tournament player should know about even if he does not actually wish to use them himself.

You will find here some new ideas which are likely to become more popular over the next few years, while one or two well-known conventions whose popularity is on the wane have been omitted.

To a degree, the choice inevitably reflects the personal prejudices of the author. Given the number of conventions in existence, it is almost impossible that any two experts would come up with exactly the same list. If I have omitted one of your pet conventions, my apologies, but then you do not need to read about something which is already so close to your heart. And if there is something here which you consider to be useless, rest assured that there will be plenty of other readers who hold the opposite view.

Each convention is described in sufficient detail that you should understand what is going on if your opponents use it against you or to allow you to give it a try yourself. I do not intend to cover every possible auction in all circumstances, rather give the basic structure plus a general overview. If you decide that a particular convention is worth adding to your system, you may need to discuss with partner some of the more exotic possibilities in the later auction.

I will also, on occasion, point out a particular strength or weakness of a method relative to the alternatives available, though the reader may often be left to work this out for himself by referring to the introduction to each section. But, at the end of the day, it is up to you what you choose to play and what not.

Part 1
The Uncontested Auction

One of a Minor

If playing a four-card major, weak no-trump system, there is no particular need for a one of a minor opening to be other than natural, i.e. promising at least four cards. However, five-card major systems, and many strong no-trump players, need a way in which to open the bidding with awkward hands that don't fit in elsewhere. Accordingly, one or both minors are played as 'prepared' openings.

Better Minor

Better minor means exactly what it says; with a balanced hand outside the no-trump range, the opening bid is made in the better minor, even though that may mean bidding a three-card suit.

Modified Better Minor

In Modified Better Minor, 1♢ is only opened with precisely 4-4-3-2 shape, to avoid opening 1♣ on a doubleton, otherwise the prepared bid is 1♣, even with four diamonds and three clubs. Other players would still open 1♢ with that hand but open 1♣ with 3-3 in the minors even with substantially stronger diamonds than clubs. Different players have different styles in this area, covering the full range of possibilities, and they will almost all claim to be playing Better Minor when many of them are clearly not doing so.

Prepared Club

The Prepared Club means that the opening bid on these hands is always 1♣, i.e. 1♢ is always a natural bid. It may churn your stomach to have to open 1♣ with a small doubleton, but it does make your bidding after a 1♢ opening a lot easier, so there is a significant pay-off to balance the obvious loss when you open 1♣. Not only does 1♢ promise four cards, but also 1♢ – 2♣ – 2NT is no longer needed to show a weak no-trump type – all of those start with 1♣. This is a significant improvement, as rebidding 2NT with a weak no-trump is a quite unattractive prospect – not only does it oblige you to play 1♢ – 2♣ as promising at least 11 HCP, but also, after the 2NT rebid, how is responder to know when to bid game and when not when holding 11 or 12 HCP?

Walsh

There are several artificial responses of 2♣/♢ over 1♣/♢ and 1♢ over 1♣ in existence, but frankly I see very little point in them. Natural bidding generally works at least as well without any worries about remembering the system. One idea that does make some sense is Walsh.

One of the perennial problems associated with playing a prepared club is the question of whether to rebid 1NT to show the general hand-type or to bid a four-card major at the one level despite having a balanced hand. If you choose the latter approach, how is partner ever to know whether or not 1♣ – 1◇ – 1♡ / ♠ includes a genuine club suit? Walsh is an attempt to reduce the scale of this problem.

The idea is that, if responder is only worth one bid, he bids a four-card major if he has one even with longer diamonds. If instead he responds 1◇, he is known not to hold a four-card major unless he is strong enough to bid it anyway on the next round, so opener can afford to rebid 1NT to show his balanced hand whether or not he has a major. So a responder with 2-4-5-2 shape would bid 1♣ –1♡ with a weakish hand, then pass a 1NT rebid, but with 11+ HCP would respond 1◇ then bid 2♡ (forcing for one round) over a 1NT rebid. This is not perfect but, as I believe that letting partner know about your general hand-type is very important, I would suggest that it is the best compromise available.

Inverted Minor-suit Raises

The idea here is to play that 1♣ – 3♣ is pre-emptive, a weak hand with good trump support and distribution but not very much high-card strength, while 1♣ – 2♣ is forcing for one round, just as if any other suit had been opened. Likewise, of course, 1◇ – 2/3◇. The less natural the opening bid, the more sense it makes to play this way, though even when one of a minor promises four cards there is a fair case for playing pre-emptive raises as, if you have a fit in a minor, the opposition may well have a fit in a major to be shut out. Also, in traditional bidding, there is no forcing raise in a minor suit. Opposite a 1◇ opening, a hand such as:

♠ A K 6
♡ 6 5 3
◇ A Q 10 5
♣ K 8 2

has no sensible response. If 2◇ is forcing, you can hear what kind of hand partner holds at a convenient level.

After say, 1◇ – 2◇ (inverted), should opener bid a four-card major with a balanced hand or rebid in no-trump? The latter makes more sense. If responder has a four-card major he must be strong enough to bid it over a 2NT rebid, otherwise he would have responded in the major in the first place. If he does not have one, there is no point your bidding it, unless you have a shapely hand and want to tell him so.

Minor-suit Swiss

This is another solution to the lack of a forcing raise of a minor-suit opening. There are a number of variations, as with most conventions. One possibility is that:

1♣ – 3◇ = 12/13 HCP and a club fit
1♣ – 3♡ = 14/15 HCP and a club fit
1◇ – 3♡ = 12/13 HCP and a diamond fit
1◇ – 3♠ = 14/15 HCP and a diamond fit

All these bids are forcing to 3NT or four of the minor, though in practice it is rare to stop out of game.

Other variants have all the three-level responses as showing opening values and a fit plus four cards in the suit bid, or just the lowest stopper. However you play around with the bids, Minor-suit Swiss is a pretty ungainly animal. It uses up a lot of bidding space to give a rather imprecise message. Better to play inverted raises or, failing that, just bid naturally but occasionally invent a bid in a three-card holding in the other minor to hear partner's natural rebid at a convenient level.

Strong Club Systems

A very popular tournament method is to play a system where a 1♣ opening is strong and artificial, either 16+ or 17+ HCP, just as a 2♣ opening is artificial in standard methods. This obviously creates a problem showing hands that would otherwise open 1♣, and puts extra strain on the 1◇ opening. Particularly when also playing five-card majors, some pairs even have to open 1◇ with a void! While this may sound strange, it does have some plus features in the freedom it allows in the rest of the system. I would not recommend such a style to a casual partnership, however.

There is no room here to go into great detail about strong club systems, of which there are many. A couple of ideas to help after the 1◇ opening are, however, to play that:

1◇ – 1♡ – 2♠ = A raise to 3♡ with an unspecified singleton or void
1◇ – 1♠ – 2NT = A raise to 3♠ with an unspecified singleton or void
1◇ – 1♡ – 2NT = 5-5 in the minors and a maximum
1◇ – 1♠ – 3♡ = 5-5 in the minors and a maximum

In the first two sequences, the next bid up can ask which shortage is actually held. This idea uses two bids which are pretty well redundant in a natural sense, because of the failure to open with a strong club, to improve your accuracy when deciding whether to bid game. As the cost is low, the idea is a good one.

The second two sequences help to show an awkward hand-type. Because the 1◇ opening may be based on a diamond suit, a club suit, or both, there are insufficient natural rebids available to show all the possible hands properly. While a trifle unwieldy, they are still better than nothing and again the cost, except in memory strain, is negligible.

One of a Major

Four- or five-card majors – another of those perennial questions. The trend is definitely towards five-card openings, but four-card majors still have a substantial following and some definite advantages to balance the disadvantages, most of which come in competitive auctions.

There are an unbelievable number of different methods in use, in particular when it comes to raising partner's suit, and I have no intention of trying to list them all. As usual, however, here are the best and the most popular.

The Forcing No-trump

When playing five-card majors, a popular idea is to play a 1NT response as forcing for one round. This helps responder enormously in describing his hand but has one significant weakness – the opener has to find a rebid even when he would prefer to pass, making a final contract of 1NT impossible and forcing him to bid a three card suit on occasions. A 5-4-2-2 hand is quite happy to rebid, as it always intended to show the second suit (at least, if that suit is lower ranking than the first one), but what about 5-3-3-2? Normally, this shape would either pass or raise no-trump. Hands that would otherwise have passed, must now bid a three-card suit. The normal agreement is to bid the lower three-card suit, irrespective of their relative strengths. Hence, a 5-3-3-2 hand rebids 2♢, while 5-3-2-3 and 5-2-3-3 both bid 2♣.

After 1♠ – 1NT – 2♣ – ?

2♢/♡	=	Long suit but a weakish hand
2♠	=	A poor raise to 2♠, usually only doubleton support
2NT	=	Balanced 11/12
3♣	=	Invitational
3♠	=	Balanced three-card raise, invitational

It is also possible to give meanings to jumps to 3NT and four of a suit. For example, an immediate bid of 4♢ could show a game raise with a diamond singleton; 1NT followed by 4♢ could show the same strength but a diamond void. What scheme you favour is not so important as the fact that the forcing no-trump has given you the possibility of showing twice as many different hand-types. Note that an immediate 1♠ – 3♠ is now known to be distributional, and an immediate 1♠ – 2NT can be used to show a forcing spade raise, a balanced 16+, or whatever takes your fancy. The advantages are very significant, but the price is also quite high. However, the forcing no-trump is quite popular amongst serious tournament players so the overall expert view seems to be in its favour.

Granville

When playing the forcing no-trump, this convention inverts the meanings of 1♠ and 1NT in response to a 1♡ opening. 1♡ – 1NT now promises five spades and 1♡ – 1♠ is the forcing no-trump type and may include four spades. 1♡ – 1♠ – 1NT shows four spades but not enough to reverse with 2♠. Again, opener has to rebid a three-card minor with a 5-3-3-2 hand.

The Jump Shift

Traditionally, a jump shift has shown a strong hand with a strong suit, usually 16+ HCP. Used properly, this is certainly an aid to slam bidding, as the alternative is a simple response then keep bidding round the houses to make forcing bids. Some players, however, think that strong jump shifts come up so rarely that it is worth giving them up and playing **weak jump shifts** instead. These can be played over an opening bid in any suit and show a hand similar to a weak two bid. For example, 1◇ – 2♠, might be:

(a) ♠ K Q J 10 8 5   (b) ♠ Q J 9 7 5 3
    ♡ K 6   ♡ 8 6
    ◇ 5 3   ◇ 7 4
    ♣ 10 4 2   ♣ Q 9 4

There are two styles to these weak jumps. In the more constructive style, (a) would be a maximum and (b) minimum; in the other, more aggressive, style, (a) would be far too good and (b) would be close to a maximum.

The idea in each case is to let partner know about your hand but, more importantly, to pre-empt the opposition. The weaker your hand, the more likely you are to want to pre-empt, but my personal view is that the weaker aggressive style is unsound, far too often leading to your playing the wrong partscore. The more constructive style, meanwhile, can be used to aid your own bidding as well as pre-empting the opposition. If a jump shift is weak, then we can play 1◇ – 1♠ – 2♣ – 2♠ – as invitational and a 3♠ rebid as forcing.

I am undecided about weak jump shifts. They are at their most effective opposite a 1♣/◇ opening which will often be a weak no-trump type. When playing a weak no-trump system, the 1♣/◇ opening will either be strong or distributional, and in neither case will you be quite so happy to hear partner pre-empt you. Perhaps the decision should be made according to your current style when using strong jump shifts. If you use them quite a lot, you will find the price of giving them up too high; if you rarely jump shift, then you will hardly miss them.

Transfer Jump Shifts

Transfer Jump Shifts allow you to have your cake and eat it, in that they can be played as two-way, either strong or weak. Because a bid like

$1\diamondsuit - 2\diamondsuit$ is needed in a natural sense, there is no spare bid to start the transfers until you get to 2NT. Now, $1\diamondsuit / \heartsuit / \spadesuit - 2NT$ can show clubs, either 16+ or 6-9, or whatever range you like for your weak version. If happy to play there opposite the weak type, opener simply completes the transfer by bidding 3♣. Responder bids again with the strong hand but passes if weak. The transfers continue, of course. 1♠ – 2NT = clubs; 1♠ – 3♣ = diamonds; 1♠ – 3$\diamondsuit$ = hearts; 1♠ – 3$\heartsuit$ = spades; always either weak or strong.

While this all looks very wonderful, in practice it makes constructive bidding more difficult than normal so there is certainly a price to pay. Personally, I would prefer to keep my jump shifts as having only a single meaning.

Baron 2NT and 3NT

Balanced responding hands in the 16+ range are awkward to show. The Baron 2NT response is an attempt to cater for them. The idea is that a 2NT response shows 16+ HCP and opener rebids naturally, with both players bidding four-card suits in search of a fit until 3NT is reached. With 16-18, responder will not be the one to go beyond 3NT, other than to support partner's suit; with 19+ he must be careful to cuebid or raise to 4NT to show his extra values. For example:

♠ K 10 5
♡ K Q J 7
$\diamondsuit$ K 6
♣ A J 8 4

Partner	You
1♠	2NT
3$\diamondsuit$	3♡
3♠	4♠

You have shown 16+ balanced, then four hearts, then a minimum with secondary spade support. Change the ♣J into the ♣K and you would bid 4♣ over 3♠; not to show the four card club suit, but as a cuebid in support of spades. The cuebid shows extra values. Partner can now judge whether to continue.

A 3NT response to the opening bid can be used to show 13-15 with four-card support for the opener's suit. This goes well with pre-emptive game raises and splinters, for example, to create a unified system of raises to game.

Swiss

Swiss was the earliest solution to the need for a strong, as opposed to distributional, raise to four of a major. Inevitably, there are several versions, most just utilising responses of 4♣ and 4◇. Possibilities are that the two bids show different high-card ranges, say 13/14 and 15/16 respectively, or perhaps that both show sound opening bids, one with good trumps and one with weaker trumps. Or the difference could be in the number of aces held. The bids used are not needed in a natural sense so the cost is low and, were there not better solutions to the problem, Swiss would therefore be a good idea. If you want something simple, then at least the above versions fit the bill. As a general principle, it is better for 4♣ to show the slightly more encouraging of the two options as it leaves more space in which to explore.

Fruit Machine Swiss

Probably the most popular version in use in today's tournament world. 4♣ shows a high-card raise with two aces plus either a third ace, the king of trumps or an unspecified singleton. 4◇ shows a high-card raise which does not qualify for 4♣.

If interested, opener can bid 4◇ over 4♣ to ask which version is held.

1♠ – 4♣ – 4◇ – 4♠	= King of trumps
4NT	= Three aces
4♡	= Singleton heart
5♣/◇	= Singleton in bid suit

1♡ – 4♣ – 4◇ – 4♡	= King of trumps
4♠	= Singleton spade
4NT	= Three aces
5♣/◇	= Singleton in bid suit

Fruit Machine is an improvement on the simpler versions already mentioned, but the restriction of only being able to show a singleton if holding two aces is a serious flaw.

Super Swiss

Probably the most complex version to actually carry the name Swiss, Super Swiss allows responder to show a singleton or void irrespective of the number of aces held.

1♡ – 3♠	= Unspecified void
1♡ – 3NT	= Unspecified singleton
1♡ – 4♣	= Two or three aces, no shortage
1♡ – 4◇	= Less than two aces, no shortage
1♠ – 3NT	= Unspecified void
1♠ – 4♣	= Unspecified singleton
1♠ – 4◇	= Two or three aces, no shortage
1♠ – 4♡	= Less than two aces, no shortage

It would be possible to swap round the void- and singleton-showing bids if you wished, on the basis that singletons come up much more often than voids. Indeed, I would strongly recommend such a switch. Also, the two ace showing bids could be used to show good and bad trumps instead or, perhaps, up to four controls, and five plus controls.

Where responder has shown a shortage opener may, if interested in slam, bid the next step up to ask which shortage is held. Responder bids the suit of the shortage or, if short in the suit used to ask the question, bids the agreed trump suit. For example:

1♠ − 3NT − 4♣ − 4◇/♡ = Void in bid suit
4♠ = Void in clubs

Super Swiss is a big impovement on the other versions and it is surprising how few pairs use it. Compared to Splinters, which we shall look at shortly, it loses a little bidding space in that the shortage is not always defined at as low a level. Against that, it differentiates immediately between a void and a singleton, and if opener has a poor hand he need not enquire, leaving the opening leader unaware of which shortage is held.

Splinter Bids

Splinter bids are a very simple idea. A double jump shift (1♠ − 4♣/◇/♡ and 1♡ − 3♠/4♣/◇) shows a constructive game raise with a singleton or void in the suit bid. Their purpose is to help opener to judge whether his high cards are working well or not. Good holdings opposite a singleton are Axx, xxx, or xxxx. Bad holdings include KQx, KJxx, and AKQ. The point is that small cards can be ruffed in dummy, while high cards, with the exception of the ace, are not pulling their weight as they can also be trumped in dummy and are not helping to develop extra tricks as they would if facing length. So, after 1♠ − 4♣:

(a) ♠ A Q 10 8 6   (b) ♠ A Q 10 8 6
    ♡ K J 3   ♡ 8 6 4
    ◇ A 7   ◇ A 7
    ♣ 8 6 4   ♣ K J 3

Hand (a) has no wastage in clubs and, while slam is not guaranteed, if responder has something like 11+ HCP outside clubs, it is certainly a possibility. Opener should cuebid 4◇, showing a diamond control and slam interest. If responder has the ♡A he will cuebid in turn and opener can make a further move.

Hand (b) has substantial club wastage, making slam much less likely. Not only is the ♣A probably missing, but opener has three small hearts, a suit in which responder will also have some length. Accordingly, responder will need much greater high-card strength to cover all of opener's losers than when he held hand (a). This time, opener should sign-off in 4♠.

The standard range for a Splinter Bid is around 11-14 HCP. With 15/16, there is a temptation to bid on even if opener signs-off, risking going down at the five level. Hands in this range are better advised to take a different route and hope to judge from partner's actions whether it is wise to go beyond game. Once responder has 17+, he can probably afford to go to the five level opposite a sign-off so it is once again OK to splinter.

One other point. It is best to avoid splintering in a suit where a singleton top honour is held. The problem is that partner will expect you to have a small singleton and so will devalue holdings which are made valuable by your honour. For example, the bare ace will make K-Q-x(-x) very useful; the bare queen will be excellent opposite K-J-x. If your system allows you any alternative, use it.

Splinters are an excellent idea, being enormously helpful to partner's judgement. They are best played in conjunction with either a 2NT or 3NT response to show a balanced high-card raise to game. As we will see later, they can also be used in other situations, not only when responding to an opening bid.

Jacoby 2NT

A 2NT response to one of a major is a constructive game raise and asks opener to describe his hand further. The fact that trumps are agreed at such a low level is very useful. In the original version, opener showed a singleton at the three level or a void at the four level. Four of his suit showed a minimum, while three of the suit showed extra values and therefore some willingness to explore slam possibilities. 3NT would show a balanced hand of some description outside the opening no-trump range.

It is very wasteful to use so many bids only to show shortages and, as always, there are many variations in use today. Perhaps the simplest and most natural is for opener to show a second suit at the three level or a shortage at the four level. With both, judgement is required and the texture of the second suit should be the deciding factor.

For example, A-K-Q-x is a wonderful suit but partner cannot hold a fitting honour so may be discouraged to hear you bid a suit where he is looking at three small. Equally, 10-x-x-x will be a serious liability for slam purposes and you would not wish partner to upgrade his Q-x holding on the basis that you had shown the suit. In both these cases, it might be more sensible to show your shortage elsewhere. But a suit such as K-J-9-x is ideal as you would like partner to have fitting honours and he will be encouraged by precisely those holdings which will go well with your suit. Now a bid of the second suit should take precedence over showing a shortage, and even more so if you have five cards in the second suit.

There are more complex variants around and it is even possible to arrange your subsequent bidding so as to allow the 2NT response to only show game invitational or better hands, allowing one major – three major to be played as pre-emptive. A serious tournament pair can find details of more exotic versions in more specialised works if required.

As all strengths of natural 2NT response are rather cumbersome, the price of playing Jacoby is quite low and, if playing a reasonable version (i.e. not the original), the ability to agree trumps and force to game at such a low level is very helpful for accurate slam bidding.

Bergen Raises

Bergen Raises are a complete structure of major-suit raises, originally designed for use in a five-card major strong no-trump structure, though only the five-card major part of that is essential. They also work best if playing a forcing no-trump response to the major suit opening. Here is the scheme of responses in brief:

1NT followed by three or four of opener's suit	= Limit raise with three-card support
Two of opener's suit	= 6-9 HCP with three trumps
3♣	= 7-10 with at least four trumps
3♢	= 10-12 with at least four trumps
Three of opener's major	= 0-6 with at least four trumps
Three of other major	= 12+ HCP, at least four trumps and an unspecified singleton or void
3NT	= 12-15 balanced with stoppers in all three side suits and three-card support for opener's suit

Using Bergen Raises loses all your natural jump shifts at the three level. In return, you get the ability to differentiate between three- and four-card raises and to make both mildly and strongly invitational bids plus immediate pre-emptive raises. The ability to count trumps exactly can be particularly valuable in competitive auctions. The scheme is only really suitable for use within the already specified bidding structure. If you rarely make natural jump shifts, it is quite an attractive idea. If you like to jump shift a lot, you may feel that the price is too high. Bergen Raises fit well with some form of Jacoby 2NT and Splinters.

Marty Bergen

Marty Bergen has been a bridge professional since 1976. He was a formidable tennis player, winning championships in high school and college and still plays regularly. A formidable player, who has won the Cavendish twice, his contributions to theory are well known. His two-volume work *Better Bidding with Bergen* is regarded as a classic and *Points Schmoints* and *More Points Schmoints* are equally well regarded. Apart from inventing Bergen Raises, he has assisted in the development of the Law of Total Tricks, Support Doubles and the semi forcing response of 1NT.

Mini-splinters

Yet another use of a jump shift could be to show a Mini-splinter. Using these, 1♠ – 3♣/◇/♡ would show a raise to 3♠ with a singleton or void in the bid suit. As with normal Splinters, the idea is to help partner to judge the degree of fit, this time when deciding whether to bid game. A typical 1♠ – 3◇ bid might be:

♠ K J 7 4
♡ K 6 2
◇ 8
♣ J 8 6 5 3

The shortage makes this worth a raise to 3♠, but how much nicer to be able to tell partner why your hand is worth a raise to that level.

While a useful judgement aid, few pairs play Mini-splinters in this way. For one thing, it is a waste of three bids to show the three different singletons. A better option would be to play a single bid, 1♠ – 2NT and 1♡ – 2♠ to show an unspecified Mini-splinter. Opener could now bid the next step up to ask for the shortage if it mattered to him. A plausible combination would be to play these two responses along with 1♠ – 3♣ and 1♡ – 2NT as Jacoby raises, losing only one natural jump shift in each case.

Passed Hand Bidding

If you are a passed hand, you may have different problems when facing partner's opening bid. Also, there are so many hands which you cannot hold that some responses are available to be given a special meaning.

Drury

It is part of the game to open a little light in third seat. The Drury convention is an attempt to cater for that when supporting partner, enabling you to stay at a safe level more often. Opposite a third or fourth in hand opening of one of a major, a 2♣ response is artificial, showing a constructive raise of opener's suit. The 2♣ response shows three- or four-card trump support and 9-12 HCP. In the original version, opener rebid 2◊ to show a sub-minimum opening, or one which could not consider game facing a passed hand, while any other rebid was natural an guaranteed a sound opening. After the 2◊ rebid, responder could just sign-off in two of the suit.

As usual there are other versions in use today. In Reverse Drury, 2◊ shows a sound opening and other non-jump rebids are weak. There is also a version where both 2♣ and 2◊ are artificial responses, the former showing four-card support, the latter only three-card. Drury is very popular in USA but whether it is really worth the trouble is debatable – after all, is it that clever to be able to tell your opponents that you have a fit but only limited values? Might that not just tell them that they can afford to compete and you will now get pushed to an awkward level anyway?

SNAP

SNAP stands for Strong No Trump After Passing. It can be used opposite an opening bid in any suit and is designed to keep the partnership low when partner has opened light in third or fourth seat. A 1NT response is played as showing 9-12 HCP, which helps to solve the problem but unfortunately creates a new one, what to bid with 6-8 HCP and no suit to bid at the one level. As the new problem is greater than the original one, I don't think much of SNAP as an aid to bidding.

The Jump Shift

A passed hand cannot hold a strong jump shift and, given the number of people who play some form of weak two openings, it is unlikely to hold a weak jump shift either. As to jump merely as a way of telling partner that you have a maximum pass is fatuous, we are left with some free bids of which to make intelligent use.

Standard methods are for a passed hand jump shift to be natural but also promising support for partner – a kind of fit-jump. A typical 2♠ response to a 1♡ opening would be:

♠ A J 10 8 6
♡ K 9 7 4
◊ J 6
♣ 8 3

The idea is to help partner to judge how high to go.

An alternative, which comes up more frequently, would be to play that a passed hand jump shift shows a mini-splinter, as discussed above. This makes more sense to me. The fit-jump type is comparatively rare because the values are supposed to be concentrated in the two suits – you would not jump on J-7-6-4-3, for example – and as knowledge of a shortage is at least as valuable an aid to judgement, it is better to use the bids in that way instead.

One No Trump

1NT is everyone's favourite opening bid, and as such it is very important to have a sensible structure for bidding after it. As there are no restrictions on what can be used in tournament play, there are a huge number of variations on the basic themes.

Stayman
The one convention that even beginners know.

1NT – 2♣ –2◇ = No four-card major
    2♡ = Four hearts
    2♠ = Four spades

It is normal to bid 2♡ with both majors, but you could agree to bid spades or indeed the stronger suit. If playing a full transfer system, however, you may find that it is more convenient to always respond 2♡ with both majors here.

After using Stayman, a 3♣ rebid by responder cancels the initial message and says that you want to play in 3♣.

Extended Stayman
If opener's response to a 2♣ Stayman enquiry was 2◇, denying a four- card major, responder can next bid 3◇ to ask for the better three-card major. As use of the bid suggests 5-5 in the majors, it would be possible to extend this so that opener bid his preferred three-card major at the three level with a minimum and four level with a maximum. Or, indeed, the reverse.

Stayman In Doubt
If opener's response to a 2♣ Stayman enquiry was 2♡/♠, showing a four-card major, responder who has a completely balanced hand, 4-3-3-3, but with four-card support for opener's major, may not know whether to play 3NT or four of the major. A 3◇ bid can be used as Stayman In Doubt, asking opener to rebid 3NT if also 4-3-3-3 but otherwise to bid game in the major.

Though not part of the standard convention, this 3◇ bid could also be used as a two-way bid, Stayman In Doubt but also as a way to set trumps

Sam Stayman

Sam Stayman's name became one of the best known ever in the world of Bridge, when in 1945 he described in *The Bridge World* a convention developed by his partner George Rapée. The idea was simple, replying to an opening bid of 1NT, a response of Two Clubs asks for a major suit. This soon became known as the Stayman Convention. He made many other contributions to the game including the development of Namyats (Stayman spelled backwards).

He was a member of the American team that won the first Bermuda Bowl in 1950, and won again in 1951 and 1953.

A former Editor of *Bridge Magazine*, Ewart Kempson, was collaborating with Stayman on a British version of one of his books and was rather impressed by the luxurious penthouse that the great man occupied in the heart of New York.

'Terribly expensive?' ventured Kempson.

'Not really,' Stayman replied. Detecting Kempson's surprise he added: 'I happen to own the block.'

cheaply to start slam exploration. The idea is that opener bids 3NT as before if 4-3-3-3 but has the option of cuebidding on the way if he likes his hand for play in the major. If responder was only interested in finding the right game, he will now either pass 3NT or sign-off in four of the major. If he was interested in slam, he can now cuebid without any fear of a misunderstanding.

Two-way Stayman

In Two-way Stayman, both 2♣ and 2♢ responses ask for a major. Responses are as normal except that 2NT is the response to 2♢ with no major.

While there are other possibilities, one simple scheme would be as follows:

An immediate response in a suit, other than 2♣/♢ is weak, allowing pre-emptive jumps on long suits in weak hands. The weaker your no-trump opening range, the more attractive this idea becomes.

2♣ followed by a new suit at the three level is invitational.

2♢ followed by any non-game bid, even 2NT, is forcing. It is possible to use 2NT as a relay to discover opener's precise shape.

Two-way Stayman is an imrovement on standard methods because it allows weak, invitational and forcing responses in any suit. The ability on a possible slam hand to discover opener's precise shape, or to agree trumps in a forcing manner below game, is a big help.

Puppet Stayman

Particularly when playing a strong no-trump, it can be convenient to open 1NT when holding a five-card major. Normal Stayman does not allow responder to discover the fifth card. The solution is to play 2♣ as asking for five-card majors. Over a 2♢ response, responder can now check back for a 4-4 fit. He can do this either by bidding his four-card major or by bidding the one he doesn't have, by agreement.

The more popular version is the one which allows opener to be declarer, thereby concealing his hand and making the opening lead come up to him. The scheme is as follows.

1NT – 2♣ –2♢ = No five-card major
       2♡ = Five hearts
       2♠ = Five spades

1NT – 2♣ – 2♢ –2♡ = Four spades, not four hearts
       2♠ = Four hearts, not four spades
     2NT = 4-4 in the majors, invitational
      3♡ = Four hearts, four or five spades, game-forcing
      3♠ = Four spades, five hearts, game-forcing
     3NT = No-four card major, game-forcing

This is Puppet Stayman. If it seems like unnecessary memory strain, simply eliminate the puppet aspect and have responder bid his lower four- card major over 2♢. Now you are playing Five Card Stayman. It is easy enough to find a 4-4 fit if there is one. Whichever method you choose, you have gained the ability to check back for a 5-3 major fit when partner opens 1NT. The price you pay is that you can no longer respond 2♣ on a weak hand, intending to pass partner's response. Either Puppet Stayman or simple Five Card Stayman requires a 2♣ response to be of at least invitational strength.

Smolen

If holding 5-4 in the majors and game values, responder would normally use Stayman then jump in his five-card suit over a 2♢ reply. Particularly when facing a strong no-trump, there may be some advantage in making opener declarer in four of a major.

Smolen solves this problem by the simple expedient of having responder jump in the four-card major on the second round, so:

1NT – 2♣ – 2◇ – 3♡ = FG, four hearts and five or six spades
                          3♠ = FG, four spades and five or six hearts

With three-card support for the long suit, opener bids game in it, otherwise he bids 3NT. With 5-4, responder will now pass; with 6-4, responder bids the suit below his long suit over 3NT, effectively transferring the contract to partner.

As all you have done is to swap round the meaning of two sequences, there is no extra cost relative to standard methods so Smolen is a good idea.

Jacoby Transfers

Jacoby Transfers use 2◇ and 2♡ responses to a 1NT opening to show hearts and spades respectively, at least five cards. The obvious advantage to this is in making opener declarer whenever the suit shown becomes the eventual trump suit. Of more importance, however, is the great increase in bidding accuracy made possible by the fact that transfers allow the responder many more different bidding sequences with which to show different hand-types.

If using standard methods, responder can bid a weak 2♡/♠, a forcing 3♡/♠, or start with 2♣ with 5-4 in the majors. Transfers allow these extra sequences:

1NT – 2◇ – 2♡ – Pass = To play
                        2♠ = Five hearts and four spades, forcing for one round (F1)
                        2NT = Raise to 2NT with five hearts
                        3♣/◇ = Second suit, by agreement either FG or F1
                        3♡ = Invitational, six hearts
                        3NT = Natural with five hearts
                        4♡ = To play

You can add on exotic meanings for jump rebids in a new suit, perhaps to show 5-5 hands with slam interest or alternatively to show a self-supporting major with shortage in the second suit and slam interest.

Apart from a slight increase in memory strain, the only cost of Jacoby Transfers is the loss of the weak takeout into 2◇. There are various ways to cater to weak hands with long diamond suits, though they all lead to playing 3◇ instead of 2◇. In return you get a spare bid, 1NT – 2♠, to use as you like. Transfers are a big improvement on standard methods.

Four-suit Transfers

One possible use of the spare 2♠ bid created by playing Jacoby Transfers is to play transfers to all four suits, so:

```
1NT – 2◇  = 5+ hearts
      2♡  = 5+ spades
      2♠  = 5+ clubs
      2NT = 5+ diamonds
```

In the case of the 2♠ and 2NT responses, you will see that there are two possible rebids for opener without going past responder's suit. Depending on the rest of your system, there may be marginal technical advantages to playing one way round or the other but really it is best to stick with whichever seems easier to remember; you can agree to simply complete the transfer to show support for the suit and make the in-between bid to say you don't like it, or vice-versa. Either way, if you make the in-between bid and partner bids his long minor it is to play; any other rebid is natural and game-forcing.

The ability to show a good hand with, say, five clubs and four cards in a second suit, is useful when it comes to bidding the right game or exploring slam possibilities, and four-suit transfers are very popular in tournament play.

Given that you are already playing Jacoby Transfers, the new price to pay is the loss of a natural 1NT – 2NT raise. The simplest solution is to say that 1NT – 2♣ no longer promises a major, though it is still Stayman. Over opener's rebid, responder now bids 2NT with the invitational type (some play that 1NT – 2♣ – 2♡ – 2♠ shows four spades and at least invitational values, and 2NT denies four spades).

Once you are playing Jacoby, you may as well play a full transfer system of some kind. Certainly the benefits outweigh the extra cost.

2♠ Range Enquiry

The other popular family of transfer systems is based on the idea of playing 1NT – 2♠ as a range enquiry, used on balanced hands which want to invite either game or slam, and 2NT as a relay to 3♣, bid on weak hands with a long minor suit.

```
1NT – 2♠ – 2NT  = Minimum
              3any = Maximum and lowest four-card suit
```

If responder has the game-invitational type, he passes 2NT or converts three of a suit to 3NT. Normally, responder will not have a four-card major in a game invitational hand. If responder has the slam invitational type, he can start bidding his four-card suits up the line in search of a 4-4 fit. With the stronger type, responder may have any four-card suit.

```
1NT – 2NT – 3♣ – Pass  = Weak, long clubs
                 3◇    = Weak, long diamonds
```

It is quite possible to add greater complexity to this basic structure. For example, some play that a 2NT response followed by three of a major shows game values with 5-4 in the minors and shortage in the bid suit; 2NT then 3NT, 5-5 in the minors with game values.

There are plenty of possibilities but to describe all possible schemes in detail is outside the scope of this book.

My personal preference is for this basic structure rather than four-suit transfers because I think there is scope for its evolving into a complex and comprehensive system without having to take the whole thing on board immediately. This is, however, a purely personal preference. Both basic structures are a big advance on standard methods.

Note that, whichever style you choose, you need to consider the meanings of other sequences which do not start with a transfer but are affected by the fact that you are playing transfers. For example, as both the above styles includes a way of making a weak takeout into a long minor, what sort of hand should bid 1NT – 2♣ – 2any – 3♣? Is this now forcing with five plus clubs or is it weak with long clubs and a four-card major and only started with 2♣ in hope of finding a 4-4 fit?

These meanings are both quite plausible, as indeed are others, it is up to each partnership to come to some agreement.

Texas

Texas uses transfers at the four level. A response of 4◇/♡ shows long hearts/ spades respectively. The idea is to make opener declarer while also pre-empting the auction in case the opposition also have a fit.

Texas has one potential drawback and it is a purely psychological one, 1NT – 4♡ sounds too natural and opener may pass without thinking. Otherwise, there is little cost and some definite benefit to playing Texas.

South African Texas

South African Texas attempts to overcome the weakness in standard Texas by using 4♣/◇ as the transfers to 4♡/♠ respectively. This seems sensible to me. 4♣/◇ responses are hardly needed in a natural sense and the Gerber alternative for the 4♣ response is no loss as suitable hands for its use are extremely rare (my guess is that it is abused ten times for every time it is used correctly).

Gladiator

Gladiator is a little different in that 2◇ is the Stayman bid. 1NT – 2♣ demands 2◇ from opener. Now responder can pass with long diamonds or bid 2♡/♠/3♣ to play. 2♣ followed by three of any suit would be natural and invitational. 1NT – 2◇ is Stayman, with a 2NT response denying a major and 3♣ showing both. An immediate response of 2♡ / ♠ to 1NT is natural (five plus cards) and game-forcing.

Gladiator is little played these days, the world being hooked on transfer systems. It is possible to combine the two.

Modified Gladiator

1NT – 2♣ = Five card Stayman
      2◇ = 5+ hearts, at least invitational
      2♡ = 5+ spades, at least invitational
      2♠ = Stayman
     2NT = Puppet to 3♣

In response to 2♣, opener bids a five-card major otherwise 2◇. Over 2◇, responder can bid as in standard Gladiator. In response to the transfers, which are at least invitational in strength, opener completes the transfer with a minimum but bids constructively with a maximum.

Various possibilities are available in response to the Stayman bid. The simple one is to bid 2NT with no major, 3♡ / ♠ with four cards. You could agree to bid 3♣ / ◇ to show five cards, or to arrange things to allow opener to show whether he is maximum or minimum. I leave the details to you. After 1NT – 2NT, opener bids 3♣ and responder can pass, convert to 3◇ to play, or make a further bid as suggested under 2♠ Range Enquiry.

Where opener simply completes an invitational transfer, any new suit bid by responder is GF.

Though rarely played, systems based on Modified Gladiator can be quite effective. Whether they are as good as full transfer systems is unclear, but they certainly have merit. One clear weakness is that they do not allow Stayman to be used on weak hands.

Two Clubs

Acol-style

In most 'natural' systems a 2♣ opening is completely artificial, showing a very strong hand but having nothing at all to say about the club holding. In Acol, 2♣ shows either a game-going hand or a balanced 23-24 HCP. In response, 2◇ is a negative and everything else a natural positive. The definition of positive here varies. Some players require an ace and a king, but these more traditional requirements have been gradually eroded over the years and most would now simply say that a 2◇ response denies about 8 HCP and any other bid promises 8+ HCP or an exceptional suit.

Any positive response is forcing to at least game, while even after a 2◇ response game must be reached unless opener's rebid was 2NT, showing 23-24 balanced. After a 2NT rebid, it is normal to play the same methods as after a 2NT opening.

Traditionally, a jump shift response to 2♣, other than 2♣ – 3◇ which is needed as the cheapest way to make a positive response with a diamond suit, promises a solid suit. These are so rare, however, that some would now settle for a self-supporting suit with one loser in it, such as KQJ109x(x).

A relatively little known part of the system is the meaning of a jump rebid by opener and what happens afterwards. A sequence such as 2♣ – 2◇ – 3♡ shows a completely solid suit and demands that responder bid an ace if he has one. Failing that, he bids 3NT with at least one second round control otherwise raises to game. Over 3NT, opener may cuebid and responder can cuebid his second round control in turn.

The 2♣ opening often cramps the bidding somewhat, particularly when responder makes a positive reply, but as some strong artificial opening is required there is little that can be done about this. It is possible to come up with a complex structure of responses involving transfer bids and relays and dividing responder's hands into positive, semi-positive and negative types, and this looks to be an improvement but it involves a lot of hard work and memory strain when you consider how often a 2♣ opening actually comes up. Such a method is hardly within the scope of this book.

CAB Responses

There are a number of possible schemes in which responder shows his aces first rather than his suit. The most common is CAB. Very simply, 2♣ – 2◇ is a negative, 2♡/♠/3♣/◇ show the ace of that suit, and 2NT shows 8+ HCP but no ace. Responses of 3NT and 4NT show two and three aces respectively. As the number of aces is already known, subsequent Blackwood bids ask for kings then queens.

While a fair number of people play some form of control-showing responses, I have never understood their attraction. While it may be nice to sometimes be able to discount slam immediately, it seems to me that all these responses do is to make the task of finding the right trump suit, if any, at a sensible level, that much more difficult.

Kokish Relay

The sequence 2♣ – 2◇ – 3NT is very inefficient, taking up too much valuable bidding space. The Kokish Relay attempts to get round this. Very simply, after 2♣ – 2◇, a 2♡ rebid is two-way, either natural or a balanced

Eric Kokish

Eric Kokish is a professional writer, teacher and coach. At the 1996 Olympiad in Rhodes, he asked why Australia were doing so well and one of his co-commentators replied because they were the only team not being coached by Kokish! He produced the annual World Championship books for almost twelve years. He is currently working on a major project for the Internet Company e-bridge. He still finds time to write for *The Bridge World*, the *ACBL Bulletin* and *Bridge Magazine* – to name but a few. He plays when time permits, and was on the Canadian team that finished second in the 1995 Bermuda Bowl.

hand in the 25-27 range. Responder is obliged to bid 2♠ and now opener bids 2NT to show the balanced hand-type, while any other bid is natural but showing that the heart bid was genuine.

While a certain amount of definition is lost when opener has hearts, the ability to show the balanced hand-type a level lower than normal and use your normal responses to a 2NT opening again is very useful.

Two-way 2♣ Opening

If you like the Multi-coloured two diamond opening but also like to play a natural weak two opening in diamonds, there is a way in which you can 'have your cake and eat it'. The weak two diamond hand-type can be included in your two club opening.

A two club opening then shows either a weak two bid in diamonds or a normal Acol strong and artificial type. You will need to put a little thought into how you develop the auction, but the basic principle is that responder assumes the weak type until proven otherwise. His normal response is, then, a 2◇ relay, unless he feels able to cope with the auction whichever hand-type opener actually proves to hold.

Benjamin Twos

Playing Benjamin, 2♡ and 2♠ are weak openings, and a way is needed to show strong hands of eight or nine playing tricks. The solution is to play 2◇ as the very big opening, equivalent to an Acol 2♣, and use 2♣ to show the eight playing trick type in any suit.

In response to the 2◇ opening, 2♡ is a negative and everything else is a natural positive. In response to 2♣, standard Benjamin has 2◇ as a negative and all other responses are natural positives. This is inefficient as all too often responder's positive cuts across opener's intentions and makes it difficult for him to show his suit(s) conveniently. After all, if opener has such a powerful distributional hand, it is likely that it will be far more important for him to be able to show his suits than hear about responder's. A better idea is therefore to only allow responder to make an immediate positive when holding a very good suit, otherwise he just responds 2◇ as a relay, irrespective of the strength of his hand. Now opener gets a chance to unwind at a low level. After 2♣ – 2◇ – 2♡/♠, you can use the traditional Acol bidding structure over a 2♡/♠ opening.

Both the 2♣ and 2◇ openings can also include various no-trump ranges, usually alternating between the two openings, so:

2NT =	20-21
2♣ – 2◇ – 2NT =	22-23
2◇ – 2♡ – 2NT =	24-25
2♣ – 2◇ – 3NT =	26-27
2◇ – 2♡ – 3NT =	28-29

and so on. The precise ranges shown can be varied if, for example, you want to use a 2NT opening to show some kind of pre-emptive hand.

Reverse Benjamin simply inverts the meanings of the 2♣ and 2◇ openings. My view is that it is marginally inferior as an eight playing trick hand with hearts can no longer be shown at the two level. Against that, a game hand with hearts can be shown a level lower, but this comes up less frequently.

Two Diamonds

A 2◇ opening can be used in various ways. We will look at its use as a weak two, strong two, and Roman two later.

Flannery

A Flannery 2◇ opening shows four spades and five hearts and an opening hand of roughly 11-15 HCP, i.e. not worth a 2♠ reverse after a 1♡ opening and 1NT response.

In response, partner may pass with long diamonds and a weak hand, bid 2♡/♠ to play or 3♡/♠ to invite game. Responder has two ways to bid game in a major. If he wishes to be declarer he simply bids his chosen contract; if he wishes to be dummy he bids 4♣ as a transfer to 4♡ and 4◇ as a transfer to 4♠. He may also bid 3♣/◇ to ask opener to bid 3NT with a top honour in the minor, or 2NT as an artificial enquiry. After 2◇ – 2NT:

3♣	= Three clubs
3♢	= Three diamonds
3♡	= 4-5-2-2, 11-13 HCP
3♠	= 4-5-2-2, 14-15 HCP with strong majors
3NT	= 4-5-2-2, 14-15 HCP with strength in the minors
4♣	= Four clubs
4♢	= Four diamonds

By agreement, a 2NT response followed by three of a major over a 3♣ / ♢ rebid can be to play or can be invitational. If these sequences are invitational, it is also possible, though not obligatory, to play an immediate 3♡ / ♠ response to 2♢ as pre-emptive.

Some pairs use 2♡ as their Flannery bid. Subsequent bidding is essentially the same as above. Flannery works well enough most of the time, but seems to be aimed at solving an almost non-existent problem, at least in a weak no-trump structure, and as such is a waste of a bid in my view.

Multi-coloured 2♢

The most popular conventional use of a 2♢ opening is the 'Multi'. There are a number of variations on the basic theme which is that a 2♢ opening can be either a weak two bid in either major, a strong balanced hand, or some other strong hand-type.

Type One – 2♢ = Weak 2♡/♠, balanced 23-24, or Acol Two in a minor

2♢ – 2♡	= To play opposite hearts
2♢ – 2♠	= To play opposite spades but interested in game opposite hearts
2♢ – 2NT	= Forcing enquiry, normally a good hand
2♢ – 3♣/♢	= Natural and forcing
2♢ – 3♡	= Pre-emptive in opener's major
2♢ – 3♠	= Natural and invitational, assuming partner to have hearts
2♢ – 3NT	= To play
2♢ – 4♡	= To play in opener's major

Though standard, the pre-emptive jumps to 3♡/4♡ are quite dangerous as they make life very difficult if partner happens to have one of the strong types. These bids make more sense when using another version of the Multi in which the two weak two bids are the only possibilities. When playing a version which includes strong options, perhaps it is better for 3♡ to be natural and invitational and 4♡ to play.

After 2♢ – 2♡, opener passes with hearts otherwise makes a natural rebid to show his hand-type.

After 2◇ – 2♠, opener passes with spades otherwise makes a natural rebid to show his hand-type but bids 3♡ with a minimum and 4♡ with a maximum (the 2♠ response showed heart support and willingness to play game opposite a maximum weak 2♡).

After 2◇ – 2NT, opener bids 3NT with the balanced hand and 4♣ / ◇ with those suits. With a weak two bid, the original style was to bid as follows:

3♣ = Maximum weak 2♡
3◇ = Maximum weak 2♠
3♡ = Minimum weak 2♡
3♠ = Minimum weak 2♠

There is some case for inverting the max/min showing bids. It is also possible to arrange things so that opener never actually bids the suit he holds, for example:

3♣ = Hearts
3◇ = Minimum weak 2♠
3♡ = Maximum weak 2♠

This way, the strong hand can always remain concealed. Over the 3♣ response, responder can bid 3♡ as a game invitation. It is also possible in the more traditional approaches shown above for a bid of the in-between suit, e.g. 2◇ – 2NT – 3♣ – 3◇ to be used as some kind of artificial enquiry.

Where the opposition intervene, it is important to know what you are doing. After 2◇ – Double, it is easiest to ignore the double but to play that pass shows long diamonds and suggests playing there. If the second hand overcalls in a major, negative doubles make sense, i.e, 2◇ – 2♠ – Double is for penalties opposite spades but suggests competing in hearts if that is partner's suit. Where the overcall is in no-trumps or a minor, it is normal to play penalty doubles. There are also a couple of important competitive sequences to sort out:

2◇ – 3♣ – 3♡ = To compete in opener's major
        4♣ = To play game in opener's major

If an opponent overcalls, e.g. 2◇ – 2♡ – Pass – Pass – ? Opener simply makes a natural bid with a strong hand or doubles to show a strong balanced hand with reasonable trumps. With either weak two, opener passes, remembering that his partner could have made a negative double to invite him to compete.

The Multi can be quite an effective weapon, particularly against opponents who have not properly sorted out their defence, but it can turn around and bite the user if he has not sorted out all the possibilities which may come up in competition.

Type Two

If the 2♢ opening includes strong three-suiters instead of Acol Twos in the minors, it makes no difference to the basic scheme except when opener actually has the three-suited type.

After 2♢ – 2♡, three of a suit shows a three-suiter short in the next suit up, and after 2♢ – 2♠ the same applies except that 3♡ is not available to show a 1-4-4-4 hand as it is needed to show a minimum weak two in hearts. 3NT takes over the role of showing the 1-4-4-4 hand. After a 2NT response, three-suiters are shown at the four level, again by bidding the suit below the singleton.

Where a three-suiter has been shown, responder who is interested in slam can bid the known shortage to ask for either range or controls by agreement. If, for example, the agreed three-suited range is 17-24:

2♢ – 2♡ – 3♢ – 3♡ = 17-18 HCP
                 3♠ = 19-20 HCP
                 3NT = 21-22 HCP
                 4♣ = 23-24 HCP

If you bid partner's singleton a second time you ask for controls. The responses are again in steps. If he has shown 17-20 you start at 0-4 controls, if he has shown 21-24 you start at 0-6. Either way, the steps then go up one control at a time.

It is also possible to ignore the range enquiry and have an agreement that the first bid of the singleton asks for controls. This makes more sense if your agreed range for the three-suited type is narrower.

Finally, in competition, opener with a three-suiter can double when he has the suit overcalled, otherwise he bids the cheapest suit available to show shortage in the suit overcalled.

Many pairs now play 'weak only' Multis – a 2♢ opening is always a weak two bid – as this allows them to pre-empt more vigorously without fear of disrupting their own constructive bidding. My own view is that, unless you really need to put a strong type in your 2♢ opening because it comes up quite often and will fit nowhere else in your system, the weak only idea is a good one. Acol Twos in the minors are not well-handled by starting with a Multi, particularly if including a second suit, and the three-suited type is rare and unless the minimum is kept quite high often leads to uncomfortably high contracts when responder is very weak.

Two of a Major

Acol Two Bids

Traditional Acol uses opening bids of 2♡, 2♠ and indeed 2◇ to show strong hands based on at least one long strong suit but normally just short of game values. These are often described as 'eight playing trick' hands. An Acol Two is opened when you are afraid that if you open at the one level you might be passed out and miss a game. Typical examples would be:

(i) ♠ A K Q J 8 6   (ii) ♠ A K Q 10 9
     ♡ A K 3   ♡ K Q J 10 5
     ◇ K 7   ◇ K 3
     ♣ 6 4   ♣ 7

Some players abuse the system by allowing partner to pass with a bust, but example (ii) illustrates why this is foolish. The two-suited type may produce game opposite nothing more than four small trumps in either suit. By definition, an Acol Two is forcing for one round.

In response, 2NT is an artificial negative, bid on all hands with less than 7/8 HCP. Even if you want to play game eventually, you should still start this way, e.g.

                    ♠ J 8 5 4
                    ♡ 6
                    ◇ 10 6 4 3
                    ♣ 9 7 5 3

Facing a 2♠ opening, bid 2NT then 4♠ on the next round. If you bid 4♠ immediately, partner will not be able to distinguish between this hand and a balanced hand with three kings, for example. How will he know when to look for slam?

All other responses are positive. A bid in a new suit should be based on a decent five-card suit or better, as otherwise it is unlikely that you will wish it to be the trump suit given opener's hand-type. 3NT would show a balanced 9-11 without genuine support for partner, and raises of partner's suit are natural and positive. There is an important difference between a simple and a jump raise. 2♠ – 4♠ denies an ace, while 2♠ – 3♠ promises either an ace or compensation elsewhere. The idea is to leave extra space for exploration when your hand is more suitable for slam if partner is interested.

(i) ♠ Q 7 4 2   (ii) ♠ Q 7 4 2   (iii) ♠ K 7 4 2
     ♡ A 2   ♡ K 2   ♡ K Q 6
     ◇ K 8 4 3   ◇ Q J 7 4   ◇ K 5
     ♣ 10 9 4   ♣ J 9 4   ♣ 10 9 4

Hand (i) has positive values including an ace so raises 2♠ to 3♠; hand (ii) has positive values but no ace so raises 2♠ to 4♠; hand (iii) has no ace but the ♠K and other good values are sufficient compensation so should bid 2♠ – 3♠.

Traditionally, a jump shift response such as 2♠ – 4◇ showed a completely solid diamond suit. You could grow old waiting for such a hand and, while useful when it did come up, it makes more sense to play the bid as a Splinter, showing shortage, spade support and positive values.

It is usual to play that a positive response is forcing to game. After a negative response, a new suit by opener is a one-round force while a repeat of the first suit may be passed.

Herbert Negatives

The 2NT negative response to an Acol Two is sometimes wasteful of bidding space, particularly 2◇ – 2NT, and it can also lead to an eventual 3NT contract being played the wrong way up. Playing Herbert Negatives, the cheapest response is the negative, i.e. 2◇ – 2♡, 2♡ – 2♠, and 2♠ – 2NT (some play 2♠ – 3♣ as the negative). With a positive response in the next suit up, you bid 2NT, so 2◇ – 2NT shows a positive with a heart suit. In another variant, 2NT shows a balanced positive and you would need to bid 2◇ – 3♡ to show a positive with hearts. My personal preference is for the former version.

Economical Jumps

An idea which never really caught on but which has some merit is to play a jump shift response as a natural positive but also promising support for partner. For example:

♠ K 7 2
♡ A Q 10 6 3
◇ 8 7 4
♣ 10 3

If partner opens 2♠, a 3♠ response loses the heart suit, which may be a vital source of tricks for slam purposes, but a 3♡ bid may make it difficult to show the spade support, e.g. 2♠ – 3♡ – 3♠ – ? If a 4♡ response shows this sort of hand, it solves the problem nicely. Of course, you could bid 4♡ with an extra ace if you wished; just carry on with a cuebid over partner's sign-off

I prefer Splinters because they are more frequent and knowledge of partner's shortage is just as valuable for evaluating your hand as knowledge of his side suit.

Weak Two Bids

Weak Two Bids are an integral part of most strong club systems, where strong hands are dealt with in other ways, and are becoming more and more popular in natural systems, often in conjunction with Benjamin 2♣/◇ openings. Though most play only 2♡ and 2♠ as weak, there is no reason at all not to also play a weak 2◇ opening, if you are prepared to open your Acol Two types at the one level. Though some will claim that a 2◇ pre-empt is a very blunt sword, it can cause a surprising number of problems for the opposition.

A weak two is normally based on a fair six-card suit and less than opening values. Traditionally this meant around 6–10 HCP, though some favour a weaker, more destructive approach, and are quite willing to open with a five-card suit as a matter of course. Ideally, most of the high cards should be in the main suit, as with any pre-empt, and it is inadvisable to hold a side four-card major.

Standard responses would be that an immediate raise is pre-emptive, a new suit natural and forcing, and 2NT an artificial enquiry, used on most invitational range hands. Some would play a new suit response as non-forcing or, my personal preference, forcing at the three level, constructive but non-forcing at the two level. Playing a new suit as a rescue, unless doubled, is a poor idea, making constructive bidding that much more difficult.

There are several schemes of rebids opposite the 2NT enquiry. Some bid shortages, useful if partner wishes to judge whether to play game or partscore in opener's suit; some show high-card features such as Kx or Qxx if not minimum, otherwise repeat their suit, which also helps to keep alternative denominations in the picture. The single most popular scheme is an American one – Ogust.

Ogust

2♠ – 2NT –	3♣	= Minimum, poor suit
	3◇	= Minimum, good suit
	3♡	= Maximum, poor suit
	3♠	= Maximum, good suit
	3NT	= Solid suit

The definition of a good suit will vary according to partnership style, vulnerability, position at the table, and so on. A reasonable starting point would be to say that good meant two of the top three honours or perhaps A-J-10 or K-J-10, but it is a matter for partnership agreement.

Hopefully, the response allows partner to judge what to do. If he needs further information, a new suit after bidding 2NT is usually played as natural and forcing, though this may be affected by how you play an immediate response in a new suit.

2NT Opposite Random Style Weak Twos

If you play a very wild weak two style, frequent five-card openings, anything from 2/3 HCP upwards, you may prefer to be able to split opener's hand into three ranges instead of two. A possible solution is as follows:

2♠ – 2NT –	3♣	= Normal minimum
	3◇	= Horrible hand
	3♡	= Maximum with four hearts
	3♠	= Normal maximum
	3NT	= Maximum with only five cards

Over the 3♣ response, 3◇ is an enquiry and in response 3♡/♠/NT are natural as above. Where a different suit is opened, just swap around the maximum responses to keep them essentially natural.

If you play a wide range but would never open with a side major, play rebids in the unbid major as feature showing, e.g. 2♠ – 2NT – 3♡ on:

♠ K J 10 8 7 5
♡ K J 3
◇ J 2
♣ 7 4

Transfer Responses to Weak Two Bids

A possible solution to the problem of whether to play a new suit response to a weak two bid as forcing or non-forcing might be to play transfer responses. Here are two possible schemes.

(i) 2♡ –	2♠	= Enquiry, whatever responses you favour
	2NT	= Transfer to clubs, weak or strong
	3♣	= Transfer to diamonds, weak or strong
	3◇	= Transfer to hearts, weak or strong
	3♡	= Transfer to spades, at least invitational

2♠ –	2NT	= Transfer to clubs, weak or strong
	3♣	= Transfer to diamonds, weak or strong
	3◇	= Transfer to hearts, weak or strong
	3♡	= Transfer to spades, weak or strong
	3♠	= Invitational raise to 3♠

Opener would be expected to complete the transfer, except with exceptional support, allowing responder to pass with a weak hand and bid on descriptively with a game-going hand.

The downside is the loss of a natural 2♡ – 2♠ bid and of an artificial enquiry opposite a weak 2♠. The hidden plus, an improvement in slam bidding when responder has more than one suit to consider.

(ii) 2♠ – 2NT = Artificial enquiry
          3♣ = Transfer to diamonds, at least invitational
          3◇ = Transfer to hearts, at least invitational
          3♡ = Transfer to spades, weak or strong
          3♠ = Transfer to clubs, at least invitational

This time, opener completes the transfer with a minimum but makes a descriptive bid with a maximum or with a hand which has been improved by finding a fit.

Responses to 2♡ can follow similar lines.

Lucas Two Bids

A Lucas Two Bid is a 2♡/♠ opening showing less than opening values, five plus cards in the bid suit, and a second suit of at least four cards. A one step response is a relay, asking for the second suit. Any other minimum suit bid by responder is to play. A single raise is invitational, as is 2NT over a 2♡ opening, while a jump shift response is forcing.

This is the standard version. It would be quite possible to play that new suit responses were for correction, rather than natural, making the assumption that one should play in one of opener's suits, and a single raise could be pre-emptive, all invitational hands going through the relay. Finally, while losing a little of the destructive effect, a modification whereby the second suit was always known to be a minor would make constructive bidding a little easier.

Restricting the second suit to be always a minor makes it easier for responder to find out, not only the second suit, but also opener's range. Use 2NT as the enquiry. Opener bids his minor when holding a minimum, and bids 3♡ with clubs and a maximum, 3♠ with diamonds and a maximum; a 3♣ response to the opening now becomes pass or correct.

Roman Two Bids

These were originally developed for use with the Roman Club system, which is rarely seen today, but the individual two-level openings are sometimes seen, particularly in a strong club based method.

Roman 2♣

A 2♣ opening is a three-suited hand, 4-4-4-1 or 5-4-4-0, with any shortage, in the 11-16 HCP range. In response, 2NT is an enquiry for the shortage while any simple suit bid is to play, assuming it to be one of opener's suits. With shortage, opener bids his lowest suit, e.g. 2♣ – 2◇ – 2♡ means that responder was willing to play 2◇ unless this was opener's shortage, and 2♡ showed short diamonds. Responder can now choose where to play, a bid of 3♡/♠ being invitational.

Roman 2◇

A 2◇ opening shows a three-suited hand, 4-4-4-1 or 5-4-4-0, with 17-20 HCP – this last can be extended upward by agreement. The short suit is unknown.

In response, 2♡ / ♠ are to play except opposite shortage, when opener will bid his lowest suit. 2NT is the artificial response on a good hand and opener bids his shortage in response.

After bidding 2NT, a new suit by responder is invitational, though by agreement it could be played that a bid below game was forcing, making slam bidding easier. Indeed, anyone who extends the possible range of the opening may wish to have these sequences asking for range or controls as a way to explore slam possibilities.

Roman 2♡/♠

A natural system has little need of these bids as they were created to cope with a problem in a system using canape, where the second suit bid is the longer. The bids show opening values, 11-16 HCP, five cards in the bid suit and at least four clubs.

In response, 3♣ is to play, a new suit is strong and forcing, and 2NT is an enquiry for distribution. After 2♡ / ♠ – 2NT:

3♣	= 5-4-2-2
3◇	= 5-4-3-1 with three diamonds
3Major	= Six-card suit
3Other Major	= 5-4-3-1 with three cards in the major
3NT	= 5-5-2-1
4♣	= 5-5-3-0 with three cards in unbid major
4◇	= 5-5-3-0 with three diamonds

In a five-card major strong club system, such as Precision, Reverse Roman Twos are a possibility, essentially the same except that the opening promises four cards in the major and five cards in clubs.

Tartan Two Bids

These are often used in conjunction with a Multi 2◇. A 2♡ opening can be two or three way: an Acol Two in hearts, a weak hand with five hearts and a five-card minor or, if required, some range of balanced hand (20-22) if this is not covered elsewhere. A 2♠ opening shows an Acol Two in spades or a weak two-suiter with spades and another suit, though many pairs play that the second suit is always a minor.

Responses in a new suit are usually played as for correction, i.e. to play if that is partner's second suit in the weak variety. A raise to three of the anchor suit is pre-emptive opposite the weak type but forcing opposite the

Acol Two. Most often, responder bids the next step up as a relay. Opener repeats his major to show the strong type, bids his second suit to show the weak variety, or bids 2NT to show the strong balanced hand.

Two No Trump

Minor Two-suiter

A 2NT opening can be played to show a weakish minor two-suiter independently, though it is also part of the Tartan Two Bid structure. Various ranges are possible. The real he-men may play 6-10 throughout, but this is really too dangerous when vulnerable. 9-13 is also popular, while to vary between these two ranges according to vulnerability looks the most practical compromise. Whatever the range, the suit texture should be good, with relatively few high cards in the short suits.

It is normal to play that a 3♣/◇ response is to play and 4♣/◇ are pre-emptive. Traditionally, a 3♡/♠ response has also been non-forcing, based on a long suit, though some play 3♡ as an artificial range enquiry with a one-step response showing a minimum, two steps a maximum.

The opening is useful as a pre-empt but constructive bidding is difficult when responder is strong. I would advise that 3♡/♠ should be played as forcing. If you want a more complex method in an area where admittedly it will not be used all that often, play 3♠ as natural and forcing and 3♡ as artificial, demanding a 3♠ response. Now the 3♡ bidder rebids as follows:

Pass	=	To play in 3♠
3NT	=	3♡ was natural; choose between 3NT and 4♡
4♣/◇	=	Sets trumps for a slam hunt
4♡	=	Natural but more encouraging than an immediate 4♡; opener is allowed to look for a heart slam if suitable.

This scheme does not allow you to play in 3♡, nor does it allow a game invitation in a minor, but it does make slam bidding easier and allows the right game to be reached when responder has a good major suit. If you would prefer to be able to invite game in a minor, play that the 4♣/◇ rebids are only game invitational and 4♡/♠ are slam tries in clubs and diamonds respectively.

Weak Pre-empt

2NT can be played as a weak pre-empt, i.e. weaker than opening three of a suit, either in an unspecified minor or in any of the four suits. The more options, the harder it is to defend. Against that, it becomes harder for responder also. For one thing, if opener is known to hold a minor, a

2-2-4-5 hand can jump to 4/5♣ pre-emptively, knowing that he has a fit whichever suit partner holds. If opener can have any suit, it is almost impossible for responder to add to the pre-empt as he can never have support for all four suits and sufficient distribution to afford to go jumping around.

In response, a bid in a suit which opener might hold is for correction, i.e. a 3◇ response to 2NT showing a minor is to play in 3◇ opposite diamonds but at least 4♣ opposite clubs. In this case, responder has better support for the suit he does not bid, clubs. A bid in a suit which opener cannot hold is natural and either forcing or to play by agreement. If your definition of a weak pre-empt is a truly disgusting hand with almost no high cards and maybe only a six-card suit, perhaps it makes sense for a new suit response to be to play. If a weak pre-empt merely means that the suit is shorter or weaker than normal but there could be a few high cards outside, then to play a new suit as forcing seems best. Finally, where 2NT could be any suit, an alternative approach would be for responder to always bid 3♣ for correction, allowing any other suit bid to be natural. Particularly if the new-suit bid is played as forcing, this improves constructive bidding but reduces the chance of pre-empting further with a weaker responding hand.

2NT as a Strong Balanced Hand

The traditional meaning of a 2NT opening is that it shows a strong balanced hand. There may be slight variations according to the basic system in use; in Acol the range is 20-22. It is not quite true to say that a 2NT opening guarantees a stopper in every suit, but certainly borderline hands with a flaw should consider opening one of a suit instead. Again, while not really being balanced, it is permissible to open 2NT with a six-card suit, usually a minor, with 5-4-2-2, though preferably not when holding both majors, or even with a singleton. This last is rarely the correct choice but sometimes a bare ace or king in a 5-4-3-1 or 4-4-4-1 hand may suggest that though 2NT is not ideal the alternatives are worse.

Traditional responses are that 3♣ is Stayman, just as over a 1NT opening, except that this time any rebid by responder is forcing to game, and 3◇/♡/♠ are natural and forcing based on at least a five-card suit. There is no weakness takeout opposite a 2NT opening.

Baron 3♣

An alternative use of the 3♣ response is as Baron, where opener is asked to bid his cheapest four-card suit rather than specifically a major. The theory is that all 4-4 fits are important when slam may be in the picture so to concentrate on the majors is foolish. Each player bids four-card suits up the line until a fit is found or 3NT reached. If partner goes past 3NT, say bidding 4◇ over 3♠, he is cuebidding with support for your last bid suit.

The only exception is where responder bids 4♣ over 3NT as opener has not yet denied four clubs.

Five-card Stayman

This goes by different names and there are a number of different versions, but the idea behind them all is that opener may have a five-card major and a 5-3 fit may be the correct contract. Normal Stayman or Baron only locates a four-card major. In the simplest version, opener's rebid over the 3♣ response is to bid a five-card major if he has one, otherwise to bid 3◊. Now responder can bid a four-card major in search of a fit. After say: 2NT – 3♣ – 3◊ – 3♡, opener bids 4♡ with four hearts, 3♠ with four spades but not four hearts, and 3NT with no major.

As soon as you cease to play simple Stayman, where 2NT – 3♣ – 3◊ – 3♠ gets the job done, responding hands with five spades and four hearts become a problem. One solution is to modify the responses to Five-card Stayman so that opener says whether it is worth continuing to look for a fit with his first rebid. In this version, 3♡/♠ are unchanged, but 3◊ promises either a four-card major or three spades, while 3NT denies either four hearts or three or more spades. Now after: 2NT – 3♣ – 3◊ – 3♡, 4♡ shows four hearts, 3♠ shows four spades, and 3NT denies a four-card major so must have three spades. This is the approach taken by the five spades and four hearts responding hand.

Puppet Stayman

This is a still more convoluted approach which tries to make the strong hand declarer as often as possible. As always, there are different versions going the rounds, but basically, after 2NT – 3♣ – 3◊, responder bids 3♠ to show four hearts but not four spades, and 3♡ to ask opener if he has four spades, though not necessarily guaranteeing that he has four cards himself. This works best if opener's 3◊ response promises at least one major. That way, responder can bid 3NT over 3◊ to show both majors and now opener can bid the one he holds. Responder may, of course, have no four-card major, having only been interested in finding a 5-3 fit. In that case, over 3◊ he bids 3♡, asking for four spades, but now passes a 3NT response or bids 3NT himself over 3♠ to show that he wasn't actually interested in the answer to his question.

While it takes a little more work, some form of Puppet Stayman is probably the best use of a 3♣ response to a 2NT opening. It certainly pays to make the strong hand declarer as often as possible as this makes both the opening lead and subsequent defence significantly more difficult.

Modified Baron

Though it seems to me to be more closely related to Stayman, this is usually called Modified Baron. In response to 3♣, opener bids as follows:

3♦ = Denies four hearts or five spades
3♡ = Four hearts
3♠ = Five spades
3NT = Five hearts

Over 3♦/♡, responder can bid a four-card spade suit to check for a 4-4 fit.

Flint

A solution to the lack of a weak takeout bid over 2NT, and a precursor of true transfer systems, is the Flint convention. Very simply, a 3♦ response is artificial, asking opener to bid 3♡. Now, responder can Pass with long hearts and a weak hand or bid 3♠ to play.

If opener has a very good hand in support of hearts he can bid 3♠ rather than 3♡, forcing partner to bid game. With a very good hand whichever major partner holds, he can bid 3NT, again forcing his side to game (some pairs bid 4♡ rather than 3NT, though this is inferior as it cuts across partner's intentions when he has diamonds).

If responder has diamonds and a good enough hand to want to show them, he bids 3♦, Flint. Now any rebid other than a minimum bid in a major shows diamonds, at least some interest in slam, and is natural. 3NT, for example, might show five or six diamonds and 8-10 HCP, and is non-forcing.

It is also possible to play the 3♣ response as Modified Flint, in which case 3♦ becomes Stayman. Because of the reduced space available, most of the modified versions of Baron and Stayman now become unplayable. The advantage, of course, is the ability to play in 3♦.

Jacoby Transfers

Just as over a 1NT opening, there is considerable merit in playing transfers so as to make the stronger hand declarer whenever possible. Transfer methods also allow responder to describe his hand more accurately as partner will normally complete the transfer and allow him to make a second descriptive bid at a convenient level.

Jacoby Transfers employ 3♦ and 3♡ responses to a 2NT opening to show five plus hearts and spades respectively. As normally played, opener simply completes the transfer unless he is willing to play in game opposite nothing but a five-card suit, when he can break the transfer in any way he sees fit.

While transfers are generally a good idea, there is one hand-type where responder is actually worse off than if he were playing traditional methods. That is when he holds a single-suited hand which would be interested in slam opposite a fit but not otherwise. The problem is that when opener completes the transfer he has no intelligent rebid, as a new suit would be natural.

My own view is that it is best to give up on the weak takeout part of the transfer method to cater for this. Play that opener only completes the transfer when he would have bid 3NT over a natural 3♡/♠ response. Now responder knows there is no good fit and can forget about slam. Any decent hand which would have chosen to play in the major should break the transfer, either by bidding game or, with a very good hand, cuebidding. Now responder knows that slam is a live possibility.

Full Transfer Systems

Jacoby only covers transfers to the majors. As over a 1NT opening, various methods can be tagged on to create a full system of responses.

The simplest addition is to find a use for 2NT – 3♠, and a popular solution is to use it to show five spades and four hearts, the problem hand if 3♣ is not Stayman.

An alternative would be to play 3♠ as some kind of Minor-suit Stayman, presumably always guaranteeing some slam interest. Opener would bid a four-card minor in response otherwise 3NT.

Four-suit Transfers are exactly what they sound like. 3♠ shows a club suit and 3NT diamonds. In both cases, opener has a choice of rebids. It is possible to play it the other way round, but the obvious thing is to complete the transfer with a fit and make the in-between bid without a fit. This sometimes allows you to play in 3NT after a club transfer.

Oswald Jacoby

Oswald Jacoby was a brilliant star in tournament bridge. When he went to war in 1941, he was the number one master point holder, and when he returned from the Korean war in 1952 he regained the title. He was the first person to win 10,000 masterpoints, as well as being the first to record 1,000 points in a single year.

He and his son Jim were the first father-son combination to be elected to the ACBL Hall of Fame. The first such combination to win a US National Championship, they jointly developed Jacoby Transfers and the Jacoby 2NT. Jim was a member of the famous Dallas Aces, winning the Bermuda Bowl in 1970 and 1971, the World Mixed Teams in 1972 and the Olympiad in 1988.

This is a perfectly sensible idea but be warned, 2NT – 3NT sounds awfully natural and if either player forgets there is scope for a disaster.

3♠ as a puppet to 3NT, based on one or both minors, is safer as a 3NT response retains its natural meaning. After 2NT – 3♠ – 3NT, various schemes are possible. A simple one is:

4♣ = Clubs
4♦ = Diamonds
4♡ = Both minors, longer clubs
4♠ = Both minors, longer diamonds
4NT = 5-5 in the minors

If you play 2NT – 4♣ / ◇ as natural, then a scheme such as that last one is rather redundant and you might find 3♠ as Minor-suit Stayman more appropriate, but most people still play 2NT – 4♣ as Gerber (see elsewhere for details). If 2NT – 4♣ is Gerber, how should you play 2NT – 4◇?

2NT – 4◇ to show both majors. Transfers are all very well, but if responder has 5-5 in the majors, he has some difficulty in showing both his suits and letting opener know whether he is only interested in game or is willing to consider a slam. If 2NT – 4◇ is played as 5-5 in the majors, please pick a trump suit, it can be used to leave responder in control. Opener does as he is told and responder normally passes but could make a slam move once he discovers which suit will be trumps. Conversely, 2NT – 3♡ – 3♠ – 4♡ shows 5-5 and a willingness to hear opener move towards slam if he is suitable or just pass or bid 4♠ if not interested.

Many other schemes are in use and still more are possible. One thing which all partnerships will need to discuss is how they handle responder having a four-card major and longer minor. Does this hand use Stayman/Baron and then bid the minor if no 4-4 major fit is found, or does it transfer to the minor then bid the major? In the former case, it is important to know when 4♣ / ◇ is natural and when a cuebid in support of opener's major; in the latter case, is 2NT – 3NT (diamonds) – 4♣ – 4♡ forcing or not? It is reasonable to assume that where the response to the transfer promises a fit, bidding a second suit is forcing, but is it natural or a cuebid?

It may sound very boring, but I would prefer to play traditional methods rather than try to play a complex system without ironing out the bugs in advance. One misunderstanding could cost more than the system gains over the next twelve months.

Three of a Suit

Three of a suit openings are pre-emptive, based on a long suit but with less high-card strength than is required for a one-level opening. Ideally, the bulk of the high-card strength should be in the long suit, while it is inadvisable to have a biddable four-card suit on the side. Beginners are taught never to hold a side four-card major but, while this is a good general rule, a little flexibility is permissible, particularly in third position.

In response to a three-level opening, a new suit bid is natural and forcing, while a raise may be two-way, either just continuing the pre-empt or with a genuine hope of making.

Alder Pre-empts
Alder pre-empts allow certain two-suiters to be shown and also have an either/or element which can make defensive bidding more difficult.

2NT = A pre-empt in an unspecified minor
3♣ = Weak with both minors
3♢ = A pre-empt in an unspecified major
3♡ = Weak with both majors
3♠ = A gambling 3NT opening
3NT = A four-level pre-empt in an unspecified minor

Facing a two-suiter, bidding one of partner's suits is to play while bidding one of the other suits is natural and forcing. Opposite one of the either/or bids, any bid in one of the possible suits is for correction, i.e. partner passes if you have bid his suit, at whatever level, but bids his suit if you picked the wrong one. A bid in a suit opener cannot have is natural and usually game-forcing.

Transfer Pre-empts
Here, a bid of three of a suit shows a pre-empt in the suit above. Though not universal, it is normal to play 2NT as showing clubs, while 3♠/NT

Phillip Alder
Phillip Alder is another English born player/writer who has made his home in America where he has a syndicated column that appears in more than 400 newspapers. He was an outstanding junior player, who represented both England & Great Britain in International Junior Championships. The second youngest player to attain the rank of Life Master in England, he went on to full International status in the Camrose trophy. He edited *BRIDGE Magazine* between 1980 and 1985.

openings are as in Alder pre-empts. Responder simply completes the transfer unless he has interest in higher things. A new suit is natural and forcing and all bidding follows the same lines as after a natural pre-emptive opening.

Artificial Responses to Three of a Suit

Natural responses to pre-empts are all very well but there are alternatives. The most obvious is to play a next step response to 3♣ / ♢ as an enquiry bid. There are various possible schemes of rebids and you can easily work something out. Here is one possibility which caters for the fact that partner will often be interested in 3NT if you have a good suit.

3♣ – 3♢ – 3♡ = Heart shortage, poor clubs but a diamond 'fit' in case responder really has diamonds
3♣ – 3♢ – 3♠ = Good clubs – 4♣ from responder is now non-forcing with diamonds
3♣ – 3♢ – 3NT = Poor clubs but diamond support
3♣ – 3♢ – 4♣ = Poor clubs, no diamond support
3♢ – 3♡ – 3♠ = Good diamonds. 4♢ from responder now non-forcing with hearts
3♢ – 3♡ – 3NT = Poor diamonds but heart 'support'
3♢ – 3♡ – 4♣ = Short clubs, heart 'support', poor diamonds
3♢ – 3♡ – 4♢ = Poor diamonds, no heart 'support'

This is a fair amount of memory work for something which will not come up all that often, but does seem to be a step forward from standard methods.

4♣ Enquiry

With a new suit response usually being treated as natural – though it is possible to play it as a cuebid, it makes constructive bidding very difficult – without a fit, responder has no clear way to agree opener's suit and instigate a slam hunt. One solution is to play that everything is natural except a 4♣ response (3♢ over 3♣), which becomes an artificial enquiry. Particularly in an age where many pairs play quite wide-ranging pre-empts, this has a lot of merit. A possible scheme of rebids would be:

Step 1 = Dreadful hand
Step 2 = One key card (an ace or the trump king)
Step 3 = Two key cards
Step 4 = Three key cards (very unlikely)

Any higher bid should show a void in the bid suit plus two key cards. This will also be a rare bid.

An alternative to the key card approach would be simply to divide your hand on more general lines: very bad hand, normal minimum, good hand with bad suit, good hand with good suit, or similar. Usually, responder will be able to use 4NT to ask for key cards after hearing the first rebid.

Again, while being a bit of extra memory work, some such scheme looks to be an improvement on traditional methods.

Three No Trump

As we have seen above, one possibility for a 3NT opener is to show a four-level pre-empt in an unspecified minor. In response, four of a major would be to play and any bid in a minor for correction. While rare, 4NT would be Blackwood.

3NT to show a big balanced hand is hardly the most subtle of weapons and is very rare. Also rare, though quite plausible, is for it to show a very distributional hand with both minors. The only other conventional meaning is the standard one in the Acol system:

Gambling 3NT

A Gambling 3NT opening shows a solid seven- or eight-card minor suit with little (usually understood as no ace or king) or nothing outside. While being very pre-emptive, you can understand the name as even when 3NT is the correct contract it will often be played the wrong way up, hence the use of 3♠ to show this hand-type in some of the artificial pre-empting structures. In response, partner only passes if he thinks he has enough stoppers in the other suits to give 3NT a fair play. Otherwise, 4/5♣ is for correction. There is also an artificial 4◇ response, for use if slam is a possibility. Opener's rebids after 3NT – 4◇ are as follows:

4♡ = Singleton or void heart
4♠ = Singleton or void spade
4NT = No singleton or void
5♣ = Singleton or void diamond
5◇ = Singleton or void club

Four of a Suit

Four-level openings are essentially pre-emptive, but 4♡/♠ can be quite wide-range bids, sometimes bid with a fair hope of making, particularly in third or fourth seat, sometimes much weaker. There are two conventional schemes.

Texas

Playing Texas, 4◇ and 4♡ openings are transfers to 4♡ and 4♠ respectively. Quite apart from not giving you the option of deciding to be declarer in 4♡, they have a serious memory flaw – 4♡ gets opened too often with a heart suit rather than spades and once done there is rarely any escape.

South African Texas

A much more intelligent idea. This time, 4♣ and 4◇ show hearts and spades respectively. There are two ways to play these openings. One, which will appeal particularly to pairs who have no strong two bids in their system, is simply to say that 4♣/◇ show better hands than 4♡/♠. Some single-suited eight playing trick hands can now be catered for. The other possibility is that 4♣/◇ must be either completely solid suits or possibly one-loser suits with an outside ace as compensation. The latter is more restrictive but is easier to bid opposite as it is more precise. It, of course, allows the hand with no loose kings and queens to become dummy, the lead coming up to the unknown hand which may gain some benefit from it.

In response to 4♣/◇, the transfer is completed unless partner is interested in slam. If he is, he can make the in-between bid to ask for further information. Different structures are possible now, but a simple one is that opener bids game in his suit with a minimum, jumps to five of the suit with extra length in a solid suit, otherwise cuebids, the implication being that his suit will not be solid in the more restrictive style if he has an ace to show.

Four No Trump

The normal use of a 4NT opening bid is to ask for specific aces. In reply, 5♣ shows no ace, 5◇/♡/♠ and 6♣ the ace of the suit bid, and 5NT two aces. Another rarity which is abused far more often than it is used correctly.

About equally frequent would be the alternative use, showing about 6-6 in the minors and a weakish hand.

Five of a Suit

5♣/◇ openings are just oversized pre-empts. Depending on vulnerability and position at the table, they can be quite variable in overall strength, but are all based on a very long suit.

5♡/♠ openings are another of those 'once in a blue moon' bids. They show a hand where the only possible losers are in the trump suit. Partner is asked to raise to six with the ace or king and seven with both.

Even less likely would be a six-level opening which, by agreement, could ask partner to bid seven with the ace or king. Don't hold your breath.

Part 2
The Middle of the Auction

Game Tries

After $1\heartsuit - 2\heartsuit$ or $1\spadesuit - 2\spadesuit$, a beginner is taught to invite game by reraising to three of partner's suit. Once we get past the beginner stage we discover that there are more useful bids we can make to invite game, ones which describe our shape to partner so that he can judge how useful his high cards rate to be, rather than merely bid game with any maximum and pass with any minimum.

Long-suit Game Tries

The most popular and most natural form of game try is to bid a second suit. After $1\heartsuit - 2\heartsuit$, the trump suit is already settled, though no-trump is still a consideration, so any new suit bid is merely an aid to partner's judgement. If opener rebids $3\clubsuit$, and responder holds:

	(a)		(b)
	♠ K J 3		♠ 9 6 3
	♡ J 6 3 2		♡ Q J 6 2
	◇ Q J 8		◇ J 8 3
	♣ 9 6 3		♣ K J 3

Hand (a) has only one jack in partner's suits. As he must be short in at least one of the unbid suits, some of the spade and diamond honours will prove to be wasted and this hand should sign-off in $3\heartsuit$, despite the near maximum for the initial response.

Hand (b) has the same shape and high cards but this time only one jack is outside partner's suits. With most of the high cards working well, this hand should bid game.

As responder is going to look carefully at his holdings in the two suits bid by opener, a certain intelligence is required when selecting a suit in which to make a game try. Holding:

> ♠ Q 10 9 8 6
> ♡ 7
> ◇ A 6 3
> ♣ A K Q 2

A $3\clubsuit$ game try after $1\spadesuit - 2\spadesuit$ is short-sighted. Partner's club holding is irrelevant and, as he is almost certain to have a poor holding in the suit, he will often downgrade hands which are in fact quite suitable for game. The intelligent try is $3\diamondsuit$, a suit where partner's holding is significant.

So what we are really saying is that long-suit game tries should really be help-suit game tries. They are still based on length, but maybe only three cards and never a solid holding in the suit bid.

Short-suit Game Tries

A reasonable alternative is for opener to rebid his short suit. This time, instead of wanting fitting high cards, responder should be encouraged by a holding such as three or four small in the game-try suit, meaning that none of his high cards are wasted.

There is little to choose between the two types of game try in accuracy, as they are merely approaching the same problem from different directions. Some hands will prove to be more convenient for one type, some for the other. Alas, you cannot play both at the same time – or can you?

Two-way Game Tries

Two-way game tries attempt to have the best of both worlds. After 1M – 2M, a new suit at the three level is a short-suit game try, as is 1♡ – 2♡ – 2NT, with spades the short suit. With a long-suit try opener bids the next step up, forcing responder in turn to bid the next step. Now:

1♡ – 2♡ – 2♠ – 2NT – 3♣ = Club suit
                     3♢ = Diamond suit
                     3♡ = Spade suit

1♠ – 2♠ – 2NT – 3♣ – 3♢ = Diamond suit
                    3♡ = Heart suit
                    3♠ = Club suit

So opener can have the best of both worlds and make either a long or a short suit game try as seems appropriate. The price is the loss of the natural 2NT rebid on a balanced 17-18 or so. That may seem a small price to pay, given that a major-suit fit has already been found, but I think it is actually quite a serious loss. Consider that there are still many hands which are not really suitable for either a long or a short-suit try, all that you want is to know if responder is maximum or minimum. You could go back to the beginner's approach of reraising to three of your suit, but that is better played as pre-emptive. Also, it is quite common to raise 1M – 2M on only three card support, even when playing four-card major openings. It makes a lot of sense to say that a game try in a new suit guarantees five cards in the first suit and therefore an eight-card fit, while 2NT suggests only a four-card suit most of the time and brings no-trump back into the picture as a possible final resting place.

Crowhurst

Whether a 1NT rebid is played as wide-range (e.g. 12-16), when some artificial enquiry is essential, or narrow range (e.g. 12-14 or 15-17), it is very useful for responder to have an enquiry bid available to discover opener's range and to check back for a 5-3 fit in either of the bid suits.

Crowhurst is a popular tool in this situation. After 1x – 1y – 1NT, 2♣ says nothing about clubs but asks opener to describe his hand further.

Say the bidding has begun 1♡ – 1♠ – 1NT – 2♣:

2♢	=	Minimum, four hearts, not three spades
2♡	=	Minimum, five hearts
2♠	=	Minimum, three spades
2NT	=	Maximum, four hearts, not three spades to an honour
3♣/♢	=	Rare, but maximum and natural
3♡	=	Maximum, five hearts
3♠	=	Maximum, three spades to an honour
3NT	=	Maximum, five hearts and three spades

With five hearts, three spades and a minimum, it is a matter for partnership agreement which feature to show. My personal preference is to bid the lower one, as partner can then conveniently rebid his own five-card suit to check for a fit.

Other schemes are possible. Some rebid 2NT with all maximums and leave responder to check again for a 5-3 fit. This has some merit as responder may not always be interested in opener's shape but be going through Crowhurst to show his own hand. A 3♡ rebid, for example, may cut across his intentions.

The point here is that, just like transfers over 1NT, Crowhurst allows you an extra range of sequences, so:

1♡ – 1♠ – 1NT – 2♣ – 3any is invitational, while 2♣ followed by the same bid would be forcing. There is one exception, a jump to 3♣ being to play, based on a weak hand with four spades and six clubs.

Clearly, if responder was intent on showing a strong 5-5 in spades and diamonds, a 3♡ response to 2♣ could make life awkward for him. Nonetheless, many pairs prefer the initial sceme as outlined above as, in practice, the problems come up very rarely.

A third possibility, particularly attractive for those playing a wide-range 1NT rebid, is to divide opener's hand into three ranges. Now a minimum bids two of a suit, a maximum bids at the three level, and all middle range hands bid 2NT.

That is quite an intelligent approach, though I should say in passing that I believe the wide-range rebid to create more problems than it solves unless your basic system structure makes its use unavoidable.

New Minor Forcing
After 1♣/♢ – 1any – 1NT, a bid of the unbid minor can be played as a checkback, looking in particular for a four-card major, though it can also

be used in a wider sense, becoming very like the Crowhurst 2♣ bid in scope.

Both Minors Forcing

Another option is to play both 2♣ and 2◇ rebids as artificial. In this case, 2♣ is the bid on some weak hands and on invitational hands, while 2◇ is game-forcing.

Because 2◇ is game-forcing, there is no need for the opener to show his range if playing a normal-style rebid where that range is only 12-14 or 15-17. He simply makes a natural descriptive bid, choosing 2NT with no extra distribution to show.

Over 2♣ opener can show a maximum by bidding 2NT, over which partner can sign-off in three-of-a-minor with a weak hand, or explore further to find the best game contract. With a minimum, opener makes a descriptive bid below 2NT, choosing 2◇ with no major-suit feature to show. Now we see one benefit of responder splitting his enquiries between 2♣ and 2◇. When opener shows his minimum, responder can choose to pass any two-level response to the enquiry bid, which will usually mean stopping a level lower than pairs playing alternative methods.

Jump Reverses

As a reverse, such as 1♣ – 1♠ – 2◇/♡ is considered to be forcing these days, a jump reverse, e.g. 1♣ – 1♠ – 3◇/♡, becomes redundant in a natural sense. The best use for these bids is as a mini-splinter, showing a singleton or void in the bid suit and a limit raise to three of partner's suit. As always, splinters are a very powerful aid to judgement and in this case can help responder to judge when to bid game on slender values and when not. There is also a negative inference available, of course. When opener fails to make a jump reverse, but merely raises directly to three of responder's suit, he is known to be more balanced, or at least, if he does have a singleton in a suit in which he could have splintered then it must be an unsuitable one such as bare ace or king.

Lebensohl After a Reverse

Lebensohl is usually seen in competitive auctions and will be dealt with more thoroughly in a later section of this book. The principle, however, can be used to solve an awkward problem in standard methods in constructive auctions.

Say the bidding begins 1♣ – 1♠ – 2♡; in traditional methods only jumps and bids in the fourth suit are now forcing, simple preference, 2NT, or a repeat of responder's first suit, are passable. This makes constructive bidding of good hands difficult, as responder has to bid the fourth suit very often when he would prefer to make a descriptive bid. The Lebensohl principle can alleviate the problem, at the cost of one of the non-forcing bids.

There is a case for always using the next step up as the artificial bid, but that is for serious partnerships to work out. We will look at the simplest case, where 2NT becomes an artificial relay, requiring opener to bid 3♣. Now:

1♣ – 1♠ – 2♡ – 2♠ = Forcing or not, by agreement
2NT = Relay to 3♣
3♣ = Natural and forcing
3♦ = Fourth suit
3♡ = Natural and forcing
3♠ = Natural and forcing

If responder bids the 2NT relay, opener bids 3♣ as requested unless he is strong enough to insist on game, in which case he makes a further descriptive bid. Otherwise he bids 3♣ and responder can pass with clubs but a weak hand, bid 3♡ non-forcing, 3♠ invitational. By agreement, immediate and delayed bids of 3NT or of the fourth suit (in this case 3♦) can show different hand-types. An immediate 3♦ might, for example, have slam interest while a 3♦ bid after using the 2NT relay might only be interested in game.

The loss of a natural non-forcing 2NT rebid is significant, but the benefits probably outweigh the cost.

Majex

To have to bid 1♠ – 1NT – 3♡ merely to force to game is inconvenient as it is crucial for responder to know whether he is facing a four- or a five-card heart suit. Majex solves this problem by way of a artificial 3♣ rebid for use on game-going hands with both majors. This leaves our initial sequence as showing at least 5-5 in the two suits but only an invitational hand.

After 1♠ – 1NT – 3♣, responder bids:

3♦ = Neither three spades nor four hearts
3♡ = Four Hearts
3♠ = Three spades
3NT = Five hearts

Over 3♦, opener can bid 3♡ with five to check for a 5-3 fit. If responder shows hearts or spades but opener rebids 3NT, he shows that he actually had clubs all along and was not interested in hearts.

As always, different versions of the basic idea are possible.

Wolff

After 1x – 1y, a 2NT rebid shows a strong hand, just short of enough to force to game. In standard methods, any rebid by responder except a repeat of his first suit is forcing. It would be nice to be able to make both forcing and non-forcing bids in any suit. This, the Wolff sign-off allows you to do. After 1x – 1y – 2NT, 3♣ asks opener to bid 3y with three-card support, otherwise 3◇. Responder can now pass, repeat his first suit, or bid a second, lower ranking suit, to play. 3NT would mean that the 3♣ bid was natural and forcing all along. It follows that any suit bid over 2NT other than 3♣ becomes forcing, including a repeat of responder's first suit.

Fragments and Splinters

We have seen Splinter bids in various situations. Any jump in a new suit, where a bid of the same suit at a lower level would have been forcing, can be played as a splinter. For example, 1♡ – 1♠ – 4♣/◇ show raises to 4♠ with a singleton or void in the bid suit. If you happen to play that a change of suit is forcing, e.g. 1♡ – 1♠ – 2♣/◇, then a jump to 3♣/◇ is unnecessary in a natural sense so could be used as a mini-splinter, a raise to the three level with shortage in the bid suit.

Fragment Bids are just the same principle tackled from the opposite direction. The unnecessary jump shows some length in the bid suit as well as support for partner and therefore a singleton or void in the unbid suit. As both do the same job, there is little to choose between them. Most people use splinters simply because it is convenient to use the same methods in all similar situations for memory's sake, and a splinter can be either the second or third suit, but a fragment must be the third so has less universal utility.

Bobby Wolff

When he was 12 years old, Bobby Wolff learnt to play bridge by watching his parents. He went on to become one of a select band who have been both top players and administrators. He was an original member of the Dallas Aces, and has won ten World Championships, mostly in partnership with Bob Hamman. He is the only player to have won at four different levels, Open Pairs, Bermuda Bowl, Olympiad and Mixed Teams. A past President of both the World Bridge Federation and the ACBL, he still performs at the highest levels, his most recent victory being in the Seniors International Cup at the Maastricht Olympiad 2000.

Transfer Rebids After a 1NT Response

When partner responds 1NT to your 1♡/♠ opening, you often have an awkward decision to make; whether to bid 2NT with a 5-4-2-2 17-count or bid the second suit, whether to make a jump or simple rebid, and so on. A possible solution is to play transfer rebids. As usual, there are various schemes in use. Here is a simple one after 1♠ – 1NT:

2♣ = Transfer to diamonds
2♢ = Transfer to hearts
2♡ = Transfer to spades
2♠ = Transfer to clubs, at least 5-5

Responder completes the transfer unless he prefers the first suit. A 5-4 hand can now show the second suit then bid 2NT or indeed 3NT to complete the picture. A 5-5 hand can jump in the second suit immediately over 1NT to force to game or transfer then repeat the suit as an invitation. Meanwhile, single-suited hands can jump to 3♠ immediately or transfer then raise, or transfer then bid 2/3NT. And if a sequence like 1♠ – 1NT – 2♢ – 2♡ – 3♠ shows 6-4 in the majors, a partnership can discuss the meaning of 1♠ – 1NT – 2♡ – 2♠ – 3♡. Obviously six spades and some kind of heart feature. Is one sequence forcing and the other invitational, or does one show a heart weakness to help partner choose between 4♠ and 3NT.

A similar scheme is employed after a 1♡ opening.

Directional Asking Bids

Directional Asking Bids can only occur, by definition, in contested auctions, yet they seem to fit well into this section as they come in the middle of constructive auctions where game is likely.

A DAB is a bid of the opposition's suit, not as an unassuming cuebid where our side has overcalled, but in any auction where we need to ask partner for further information, in particular for a stopper to play in no-trump. Some play that a DAB promises at least a partial stop in the suit bid, but this is too restricting and it is more normal to promise nothing more than that this is the most intelligent bid available.

West	North	East	South
1♠	2♡	3♣	Pass
3♡			

This is a DAB. As 3♠ or 3♢ would be forcing, it denies the ability to make either of these bids. Unless proven otherwise, for example East bids 3NT and West removes to 4♣ (showing a club slam try) the DAB is looking for a heart stopper to play 3NT. East should therefore bid 3NT with a stopper, unless strong enough to consider slam.

With no stopper, East makes a descriptive bid. As in this kind of auction East may not know where to go unless he has the required stopper, he can rarely afford to jump to show extra values, and West should promise a further bid. In some sequences, however, it should be possible to stop short of game, e.g.

West	North	East	South
1♣	Pass	1♢	1♡
1♠	2♡	Dble	Pass
3♣	Pass	3♡	Pass
?			

East has made a competitive double of 2♡ then a DAB of 3♡. If West now bids only 4♣, East should be allowed to Pass. Most likely, West has two heart losers and East will need a very good hand to make game. It follows that West should jump to 5♣ with a suitable hand with no heart stopper. Usually, this will mean a singleton heart and sound values.

Fourth Suit Forcing

Just about the most useful single convention in all of bidding is Fourth Suit Forcing, so universally played among serious players that it is considered to be almost a part of basic bidding rather than a convention.

FSF is a big subject and can hardly be covered in depth in this volume, but the basic idea is very simple; if our side has bid three suits in a constructive auction, we are unlikely to need to bid the fourth suit in a natural sense.

Almost everybody now plays that a bid in the fourth suit is artificial, saying that there is no ideal descriptive bid currently available and asking for further information. Either opener or responder can use it. Most play it as forcing for one round, showing at least the values to go to 2NT, though not a hand suitable for that bid. Some prefer to play it as forcing to game.

The latter style takes some pressure off on some hand-types, but restricts the ability to use FSF on some others. Some eminent theorists swear that game-forcing is the correct style, but my personal preference is at least invitational, unless the FSF bid is made at the three level.

Many less experienced players say that FSF asks for a stopper for no-trump. That is NOT correct. FSF asks partner to make the most descriptive bid he can, given the information you already have about his hand; in other words, he wants to know the most important feature you have not yet shown. So after 1♡ − 1♠ − 2♣ − 2♢, holding:

♠ —
♡ Q J 9 7 6 3
♢ K 4
♣ A J 10 6 3

To bid 2NT is hardly descriptive, despite the diamond stopper. If this hand belongs in no-trumps, you will get another chance to bid them. For now, bid 3♣ to show the two-suiter.

Try another one. You hold:

♠ K Q
♡ A J 8 6 3
◇ 8 4
♣ K 10 7 4

After 1♡ – 1♠ – 2♣ – 2◇, partner already knows you have five hearts, four clubs, and less than four spades. If you now bid 2♠, as you would with three small, do you think he will really be disappointed when he sees your doubleton support?

The second part of the job of responding to FSF is to show your strength. If partner has shown at least invitational strength, you make a minimum descriptive rebid when you would decline a game invitation, but jump or make some other strength showing bid such as raising the fourth suit (except 1♣ – 1◇ – 1♡ – 1♠ – 2♠, which is natural but weak), to show extra values, enough to play in game. So after 1♡ – 1♠ – 2♣ – 2◇:

(a) ♠ 6   (b) ♠ 6
    ♡ K J 10 7 5   ♡ A Q 10 7 5
    ◇ Q J 8   ◇ K J 8
    ♣ A J 6 3   ♣ A J 6 3

Hand (a) bids 2NT, showing a diamond stopper but a minimum hand, while hand (b) bids 3NT, also showing a diamond stopper but with values to accept a game invitation.

There is a second use for FSF; it allows the user an extra range of bids to describe his own hand. Take the sequence 1♡ – 1♠ – 2♣. If responder now bids 2♡ or 2♠ they are weak; 3♣/♡/♠ are invitational. Constructive bidding is very imprecise when we have no descriptive forcing bids available. Not to worry, bid 2◇, FSF, then bid 3♣/♡/♠ on the next round. A bid which would have been only invitational if made on the previous round becomes forcing if made after using FSF. So:

(c) ♠ K J 9 8 7 6   (d) ♠ K J 9 8 7 6
    ♡ 7   ♡ 7
    ◇ A 8 5   ◇ A 8 5
    ♣ Q 10 3   ♣ A J 3

Hand (c) might bid an immediate 3♠, invitational, while hand (d) bids 2◇, FSF, then a forcing 3♠ on the next round.

Part 3
Slam Bidding

When slam is in the picture aces, and to a lesser extent kings, become very important. There are nowadays any number of options available to count aces and other key cards.

Blackwood

Standard Blackwood is probably the most popular convention in the game. It works very simply; once trumps are agreed, 4NT asks partner how many aces he holds. In response:

5♣ = 0 or 4
5♦ = 1
5♥ = 2
5♠ = 3

Unless someone's judgement has gone seriously awry, there should never be any doubt as to whether 5♣ shows 0 or 4.

After using 4NT, the same player may ask for kings by bidding 5NT. Responses are as to 4NT but a level higher.

Roman Blackwood

Blackwood tells you how many aces partner holds but not which ones. Roman Blackwood seeks to tell you that also, though only when specifically two aces are held. The responses to 4NT are:

5♣ = 0 or 3
5♦ = 1 or 4
5♥ = 2 aces of the same colour
5♠ = 2 aces of the same rank
5NT = 2 odd aces

Again, unless the response was 5NT, the 4NT bidder can next bid 5NT to ask for kings, responses being as in standard Blackwood.

Roman Key Card Blackwood

This version reflects the fact that trump honours are just as important as aces when considering a slam, and is very popular in tournament bridge. The king of trumps is always treated as an ace and the queen can also be shown or denied. The responses to 4NT are:

5♣ = 0 or 3 key cards
5♦ = 1 or 4 key cards
5♥ = 2 or 5 key cards but no trump queen
5♠ = 2 or 5 key cards plus the trump queen

A key card is any ace or the king of trumps. As you can imagine, it becomes very important that both players agree as to which suit is trumps.

Easley Blackwood

More than 60 years ago, Easley Blackwood submitted his brainchild to Ely Culbertson's magazine, *The Bridge World*, and was turned down! The magazine responded, 'While the suggestion is a good one, the 4NT bid will remain informative rather than interrogative....'

However, the convention that bears his name caught on, and by the time Blackwood published it in 1949 it had already been described in 57 books and 17 languages!

His bridge activities included looking after clients on 32 luxury cruise liners!

It was during his period in office as Executive Secretary from 1968-1971 that the ACBL became financially stable.

Of his many books, *The Complete Book of Opening Leads at Bridge* is one of the finest ever written. On 28 October 1977 the mayor of his city honoured him by proclaiming it Easley Blackwood Day.

In potentially ambiguous auctions, it is good to have some general rule to overcome any doubt.

Neither a 5♣ nor a 5◇ response to 4NT says anything about the queen of trumps. If the 4NT bidder next makes the cheapest bid which cannot be a sign-off in the agreed trump suit, it asks for the trump queen. There are two main schemes of responses in existence. The first is that the first step says no trump queen, the second says yes. E.G. 2♡ – 4♡ – 4NT – 5♣ – 5◇ – 5♡ says no ♡Q; 5♠ says yes, I do have it.

The alternative is for a return to the agreed trump suit at minimum level to deny the trump queen and any other bid to show it. The idea is that responder can also show an extra useful feature when he holds the trump queen, in case partner may be interested in seven. So, say spades are trumps: 5♠ would say no trump queen; 6♠ would say yes but nothing else worth showing; 6♣/◇/♡ would say yes and I have something useful here that you don't yet know about. This something extra cannot be an ace as they have already been counted, so is likely to be a king or perhaps a suit which is more solid than expected so will provide a source of tricks.

In fact, the first scheme can be modified to work in much the same way if you prefer it but want to add the greater complexity at a later date.

The 4NT bidder also has the alternative of following up with 5NT as a king ask. Remember that the trump king has already been shown, so don't show it a second time.

Some pairs use 5NT to ask for specific kings rather than the number held. Responder bids the suit of his cheapest king or signs-off in the agreed trump suit with none.

One other variation is that some pairs invert the meanings of the first two steps in response to 4NT. In other words, 5♣ is used to show one or four key cards, while 5♢ shows zero or three. There is some marginal advantage to switching the meanings of the two bids, but which is the better scheme depends on what suit is trumps, and the benefits are marginal. Fine, then, if you are confident of partner's memory, but not worth the risk that he might forget the agreement.

Baby Blackwood

This uses 3NT as the ace asking bid. It is usually only used over a major suit and only in auctions where it is clear that it cannot be natural. Responses are as to normal Blackwood but a level lower. There is no reason why any of the above schemes of responses cannot be used.

Kickback

While 4NT is a perfectly sensible bid to use to ask for aces or key cards when spades are agreed, it becomes gradually less convenient as the rank of the trump suit falls until it is very awkward when clubs are trumps.

Kickback suggests that a different bid should ask for aces for each agreed trump suit. The bid chosen is four of the suit immediately above the agreed trump suit. So with clubs agreed 4♢ is the asking bid, with diamonds agreed 4♡ asks, and so on.

Kickback responses are usually as in Roman Key Card Blackwood, first step 0 or 3, second step 1 or 4, etc, though any scheme of responses could be used.

Kickback is a very good idea as it saves valuable space, but you need to be very clear when the bid is actually Kickback. Let us suppose that you normally play 1♠ – 2♣ – 4♢ as a splinter in support of clubs – a perfectly sensible agreement. If playing Kickback, is 4♢ still a splinter or does it ask for key cards? If the latter, presumably 1♠ – 2♣ – 4NT is a splinter in diamonds. This is all perfectly sound, but there is scope for an almighty disaster if partner sees the situation in a different light.

Gerber

Gerber uses 4♣ to ask for aces. It normally employs standard Blackwood style responses but, as usual, there is no reason why any of the other schemes cannot be used instead.

Gerber should really only be used as an immediate response to a no-trump opening bid or in a sequence where partner's no-trump bid was the first natural bid in the auction (e.g. 2♣ – 2◊ – 2NT – 4♣). The use of 4♣ as Gerber irrespective of the previous auction is quite unsound. It is sometimes needed in a natural sense, sometimes as a cuebid, sometimes as a splinter.

DOPE and ROPE

What happens when partner uses Blackwood or, indeed, any of the other ace-asking devices and the next player intervenes. A simple sceme is that Double, or Redouble, shows an odd number of aces, or key cards, and Pass an even number. This is O.K. so long as you are confident that you will not misguess by two aces how many partner holds.

DOPI and ROPI

This variation has Double (or Redouble) to show no aces, Pass to show one, and the cheapest bid to show two. Relative to DOPE and ROPE, it is more precise but you have to decide at what level of intervention to stop playing it – if RHO bids 6♠, you hardly want to bid 6NT to show two aces.

A better version is to play that Double shows the first step (0 or 3 in RKCB) and Pass the second (1 or 4 in RKCB), but this still requires a bid when holding two key cards so has the same problem as before.

Cuebids

For all the ace-asking conventions, the most valuable aid to accurate slam bidding is the cuebid. The basic idea is very simple. When a trump suit is agreed, a bid in a new suit which commits your side to game shows a control in the bid suit – ace, void, king or singleton. A bid which does not commit you to game is not a cuebid, until clearly proven otherwise it should be read as a game try of some description. E.G. 1♡ – 3♡ – 3♠ is a cuebid, 1♣ – 3♣ – 3♠ is initially showing spade values and looking towards 3NT, though if partner bids 3NT and you now remove to 4♣ or anything else it becomes clear that 3♠ was intended as a cuebid.

Where Blackwood asks a question and you are obliged to answer, a cuebid allows you to use your judgement. Say it begins 1♡ – 3♡ – 4♣ (cuebid), and you hold:

(a)	♠ Q 7 4	(b)	♠ J 6 3	(c)	♠ A 8 7
	♡ Q J 6 3		♡ Q J 6 3		♡ Q J 6 3
	◊ K 8 5		◊ A 8 7 4		◊ K 6 3
	♣ Q 7 3		♣ K 7		♣ J 7 4

Hand (a) should sign-off in 4♡. It was barely worth a raise to 3♡ in the first place and is quite unsuitable for slam. Hand (b), on the other hand, has good controls and a potential ruffing value. Only the ♠J may be wasted. Bid 4◇, cuebid. Hand(c) would have cuebid 4◇ had the ◇K and ♠A been swapped round, but the poor shape should dissuade you from cuebidding beyond game. Sign-off in 4♡ and, if slam is on, surely partner will bid again and now you can co-operate. Give hand (c) ♠AJ87 and ♣74, and now a 4♠ cuebid would be merited.

In other words, a cuebid below game need not promise the Earth, the first cuebid above game, the first bid to actually force you to a higher level, should show a good hand for your previous bidding.

Standard cuebidding style permits you to show either first- or second-round controls, but it is usual to cuebid first-round controls before second-round. If you bypass a suit, therefore, you tend to deny as good a holding in that suit as in the one you do actually cuebid. So a sequence like: 1♡ – 3♡ – 4◇ – 4♠ – 5♣, shows first-round diamond control but only second-round club control because you bypassed 4♣. Opener has also denied first-round spade control as he also bypassed 3♠. Conversely: 1♡ – 3♡ – 4♣ – 4♠ – 5◇, could be first-round control of both minors, second-round control of both minors, or first-round clubs, second-round diamonds. The only thing it cannot be is first-round diamonds, second-round clubs.

The one suit you cannot cuebid is the agreed trump suit – you need some bid to show that you have nothing, or no desire, to cuebid, and that bid is the lowest available level of the trump suit. Occasionally, with a good hand for slam, presumably including good trumps, but no control to cuebid, you might jump in trumps rather than sign-off cheaply.

Always remember the previous bidding. If it becomes clear that you do not have the combined values to make twelve tricks, or you discover that there are two top losers, sign-off immediately. If you discover that there are twelve tricks but not thirteen, and the necessary controls are in place, bid the slam directly, don't continue to cuebid. For example, if you cuebid at the six level, partner is entitled to assume that you know all the first- round controls are present and are exploring the possibility of a grand slam.

There is no reason why cuebids and Blackwood cannot be used on the same deal; check that partner has the vital control by cuebidding, then ask for aces with Blackwood.

3NT To Start Cuebidding

Where a trump suit is clearly agreed and there is no question of 3NT being a natural bid, we have already seen the possibility of playing Baby Blackwood. Another possibility is to use 3NT as a way of saying ' please start cuebidding'. This means that after a start like 2♡ (strong) – 3♡, a new suit can be a natural slam try, showing length in the same way as with a game try after 1♡ – 2♡. A hand that wants to cuebid bids 2♡ – 3♡ – 3NT and lets partner start things off. For me, this is a much better idea than Baby Blackwood, as partner's fit or lack of same for a second suit may be decisive. How else will we ever be able to let him know that one queen is worthless and another worth its weight in gold?

The 'Serious' 3NT

A 3NT bid can be used in a variety of artificial ways in possible slam auctions. Take auctions of this type:

West	East		West	East
1♠	2♡		1♠	2♣
3♡	?		2♡	3♠
			?	

Many people, particularly those who play 'two-over-one game-forcing', treat the last bid as forcing and more encouraging than a jump to game, leaving room for cuebidding. The problem is that neither player has limited their hand. At this point, both East and West could have near-minimum hands with reasonable controls or could have substantial extra values. The next player will always want to cuebid if he has extra values, but will also wish t o do so on less good hands in case his partner is strong, as simply raising to game leaves little room for further exploration Accordingly, a raise to game in either of the above auctions would suggest a minimum hand with poor controls – one with no slam interest.

A cuebid that does not promise extra values runs the risk of partner's getting too excited and, of course, if one hand makes a cuebid then the other will also do so even if he in turn has no significant extras. The solution is the 'Serious' 3NT.

Where the partnership has clearly agreed a major suit at the three level in a forcing situation, it can be assumed that it will not then wish to play in 3NT, therefore a bid of 3NT is available for artificial use. Using the 'Serious' 3NT, if a player's first cuebid is at the four level when he had the option of bidding 3NT instead, he is just making a courtesy cuebid in case partner has substantial extra values. The cuebidder himself is a near minimum. If he has substantial extras himself, he bids 3NT, saying that he is 'serious' in his slam interest, and invites partner to start cuebidding.

So in the above sequences:

West	East		West	East
1♠	2♡		1♠	2♣
3♡	4♣/◇		2♡	3♠
			4♣/◇	

show near minimum hands but with reasonable controls – a bad hand would just sign off in game – while:

West	East		West	East
1♠	2♡		1♠	2♣
3♡	3NT		2♡	3♠
			3NT	

show extra values, say 15+ HCP or the equivalent.

If, in the first sequence, East cuebids 3♠:

West	East
1♠	2♡
3♡	3♠

then West can bid 3NT to show 15+ or cuebid 4♣/4◇ to show a control but a near minimum hand.

Grand Slam Force

Sometimes, aces are not important, or rather they are already known, and all you want to know is how many top trump honours partner holds. A bid of 5NT, without previously bidding 4NT, is the Grand Slam Force. A silly name as its use does not force you to a grand slam at all. You will not be surprised to hear that there are several sets of responses in existence. The simplest is just to bid 6♣ with none of the top three honours, six of the agreed trump suit with one top honour, and 7♣ with two.

In practice, this means that when clubs are agreed you must make the same bid with 0 or 1 top honour. A possible solution for a regular partnership is to use 5♠ as the GSF bid when clubs are agreed, leaving room for 5NT to show no honour and 6♣ one.

When a major suit is trumps, there are spare bids available. A regular partnership may agree a more complex method to utilise these. For example, you may distinguish between the queen and one of the higher honours or have a bid to show one honour to extra length.

Roman Asking Bids

An unusual jump in an unbid suit, or an opponent's suit, can be used as an asking bid to ask specifically about the suit bid. If cuebids or splinters are in use, these asking bids may be restricted to jumps to the five level. In response:

1st step = No 1st or 2nd round control in the suit
2nd step = Singleton
3rd step = King
4th step = Void

5th step = Ace
6th step = Ace and king

By agreement, the second and third steps and the fourth and fifth steps may be combined to save space. This will sometimes lose some precision but if the asking bids have to be made at the five level there may not be room for the full scheme.

Last Train

Where there is only one bid available between the last call and a sign-off in the agreed trump suit, some believe that that bid is best used as a general slam try, rather than showing a specific feature in the suit bid. For example:

West	East
1♡	3♡
4♣	4♢

In this auction, 4♢ would merely express a willingness to consider a slam but deny the ability to be the one to go past the game-level, and would say nothing about his diamond holding.

The principle can be used in many auctions. Indeed, while it is not then called 'Last Train', most players would already assume that the last call in this auction was intended as a general game try:

West	North	East	South
1♠	2♢	2♠	3♢
3♡			

Part 4
The Competitive Auction

Defences to a Strong Club

Opponents who have a well-developed system and know it have a definite advantage when they open with a strong club compared to other pairs who are playing natural methods. Left to themselves, they are more likely to have an accurate auction to the correct contract. At the same time, because they have not yet mentioned a suit, strong clubbers are also more susceptible to intervention. Although bidding may give valuable information to an opposing declarer, it pays in the long run to get into the auction over a strong club whenever possible to try to negate that advantage. Most players, particularly when non-vulnerable, will come in on less than they would have required had the opening bid been natural.

There are a whole host of artificial defences to a strong club in existence, many of them almost indistinguishable from each other. While natural weak jump overcalls are always an option, most artificial defences are geared to showing two-suiters. The simplest of these is just to use double to show both major suits and 1NT to show both minors.

This has the merit of simplicity, there is very little to forget, and also partner knows straight away which two suits you hold. If he has a fit for one of them, he can sometimes raise the auction to an uncomfortably high level before the opener has even bid one suit.

And, of course, the two calls used in an artificial sense are ones which are not needed naturally – you could hardly make a takeout double of an artificial opening bid, nor would you want to show a strong no-trump type when the opener has already shown a strong hand. Indeed, what is common to every defence to a strong club opening is that good hands pass first time around then judge whether to come in later.

Developing that last point a little further. Suppose that you pass in second seat and opener makes a natural rebid. Now you should play exactly the same methods as over a natural opening bid on your right, for example:

West	North	East	South
1♣	Pass	1♢	Pass
1♠	2♠		

shows exactly the same hand-type as:

West	North	East	South
1♠	2♠		

Likewise, if opener rebids 1NT, you can play the same defence as if he had opened 1NT.

There are two main families of defences to a strong club. In the defence we looked at above, the overcaller defined his hand immediately, his suits were known. The other family uses 'either or' or 'wonder' bids, as they are sometimes known. Here, the overcall shows one of two or more different possibilities, for example, 1NT might show either both majors or both minors. The idea is firstly to sow confusion and secondly to deprive the opposition of an easy cuebid.

The disadvantage of this latter approach is that responder to the overcall is also in the dark as to which option his partner actually holds, and this makes it harder for him to raise pre-emptively. Nevertheless, the majority of serious tournament partnerships now favour this style of defence.

Amsbury
2any = Three suiter, short in the bid suit OR touching two-suiter, excluding the suit bid OR natural and weak

Badger
Dble = Hearts and a minor
1◇ = Spades and another
1NT = Both minors

Crash
1◇ = Two suits of the same colour
1♡ = Two suits of the same rank
1NT = Two odd suits

Joe Amsbury

Joe Amsbury developed a brilliant understanding of the Acol system through his association with Bob and Jim Sharples. He passed that knowledge on to hundreds of players through his regular articles, initially in *BRIDGE Magazine* and later in *Popular Bridge Monthly*, which he created along with Tony Sowter. His partnership with Sowter was one of the dominant forces in English Bridge for many years, and involved numerous International appearances. An outstanding raconteur, Joe would usually keep his audience entertained with stories into the small hours.

Disco
Dble = Both majors
1NT = Both minors

Modified Crash
Dble = Two suits of the same colour
1◇ = Two suits of the same rank
1NT = Two odd suits

Panama
2any = Natural and weak OR three-suiter short in the bid suit

Trap
Dble = Hearts
1◇ = Spades
1♡ = Two suits of the same colour
1♠ = Two suits of the same rank
1NT = Two odd suits
2any = Natural and weak OR three-suiter short in bid suit

Trap with Transfers
As above but:

2♣ = Diamonds OR both majors
2◇ = Hearts OR both black suits
2♡ = Spades OR both minors
2♠ = Clubs OR both red suits
2NT = Hearts and clubs
3♣ = Spades and diamonds

Truscott
Dble = Clubs and hearts
1◇ = Diamonds and hearts
1♡ = Hearts and spades
1♠ = Spades and clubs
1NT = Spades and diamonds
2♣ = Clubs and diamonds

It is, of course, possible to combine two of these defences. For example, Crash, which only utilises one-level calls, could be played alongside either Amsbury or Panama, which use only two-level bids.

What I think is important, is to be able to make simple one-suited overcalls in at least the major suits. Not only does this allow you to make lead-directing bids, but also this offers your single best chance of finding a fit with partner which allows him to pre-empt the bidding further.

Alan Truscott

Alan Truscott was born in England, but has spent most of his life in the USA, having been the bridge columnist for the *New York Times* since 1964. An outstanding chess player in his Oxford days, he turned to bridge, and represented both Great Britain and the USA in world championship play. He was President of the International Bridge Press Association from 1981-86. Apart from his various contributions to theory, he invented the Truscott Card, which is now used to prevent seating errors in team events. He has been Executive Editor of every edition of the ACBL's *Official Encyclopaedia of Bridge*, and has attended every single World Bridge Olympiad!

Hence, I am not a fan of Truscott. Though this has the advantage of defining both suits immediately, it does not allow a 1♡ or 1♠ overcall to be made.

I do not have a problem with Trap because, though natural overcalls cannot be made at the one level, the hand-type can be shown via a double or 1◇ (showing spades) bid.

Responding to the Overcall

Whether partner's overcall is natural or artificial, the assumption is that it shows a weak hand, sound opening bids normally passing then coming in on the next round. Responder with a fit for the overcall should look to pre-empt as high as he can to leave the opposition with as little bidding room as possible. How high you can afford to pre-empt will depend somewhat on partner's style; just how weak can he be for his overcall?

Let us assume that partner would normally need at least a five-card suit to bid 1♠ over 1♣ – many players would quite happily bid with only four cards.

(a)   ♠ K 9 6   (b)   ♠ K J 9 6
       ♡ 10 3   ♡ 10 3
       ◇ 10 8 6 4   ◇ 10 8 6 4
       ♣ 9 7 6 3   ♣ 9 7 6

Hand (a) should raise to 2♠ whatever the vulnerability. Though this may look scarey if vulnerable, bear in mind that partner will have a better hand in that case, meanwhile, with a spade fit and no defence, you want to raise the ante as much as you can.

Hand (b) should raise to 3♠ except when vulnerable against not, when perhaps 2♠ is sufficient. Assuming a nine-card fit, you should not lose too big a penalty at the three-level and once again you want to make life as tough as possible for your opponents.

Your bidding is normally geared to pre-emption. Occasionally, you will have a hand sufficiently good that you want to invite game, yet all your raises are pre-emptive and, as the opposition have not yet bid a suit, there is no cuebid available. The solution is to use a 1NT response to a single-suited overcall as an unassuming cuebid, saying that you like partner's suit and still consider game to be a possibility.

Now, what about responding to an 'either/or' bid? Again, you want to be able to raise the level of the auction as far as possible. This time, however, you will need to have support for at least one of partner's suits whichever combination he actually holds. For example, suppose that partner overcalls 1♠, showing two suits of the same rank and the next hand passes.

(a) ♠ K 7 6 3   (b) ♠ 9 8 6
     ♡ Q 8 5 4 2   ♡ Q 8 5 4 2
     ◊ 7   ◊ 7
     ♣ 9 8 6   ♣ K 7 6 3

Again, just how vigorously you can afford to pre-empt will depend on partner's overcalling style. In most bidding situations, the term two-suiter suggests at least 5-4 and often 5-5 in the two suits. Many players will quite happily come in at the one level over a strong club on a very weak hand with only 4-4 in their two suits. Clearly, knowing partner's style here is important.

All suit bids by responder are for correction, though you may agree to exclude game bids, and you should always bear in mind that partner may not have the option you would prefer.

With hand (a), you would like to pre-empt if partner has the majors but cannot afford to do so opposite the minors. You have to respond a simple 2♣, saying that you prefer clubs to diamonds if that is what partner holds. If he converts to 2♡, showing the majors, you may make a pre-emptive raise next time around.

Hand (b) has a genuine fit whichever option partner holds. Accordingly, you can afford to jump to 3♣. This says that you prefer clubs to diamonds and are willing to play in 3♣ or at least three of one of the majors. Swap round your hearts and clubs and you might decide that you are willing to compete to 3♡ opposite the majors but 4♣ opposite the minors. The way to say this is to respond 3♡ (partner will not know which minor you like, of course).

You can use no-trump bids to ask partner to bid his longest suit, the lower with equal length. Once he does so, you will also know his second suit, of course. This would save your guessing what to do with a completely balanced hand – why guess and risk a possible 3-4 fit when there may be a 3-5 fit available in his other suit?

After 1♣ – Pass – 1♢

After partner has passed over the opposing strong club bid and third hand makes a negative response, most of the fourth player's calls can be used in exactly the same way as in second position. Some of the above defences will have to be modified a little, but none have to be scrapped completely. It is worth bearing in mind, however, that while you may well want to show the same general hand-types, it is probably inadvisable to make the very weak destructive bids much beloved by some players. the point is that partner is more likely to have a good hand than when you are in second seat, and you will make his life very difficult with such bids.

Defences to One of a Suit

The Simple Overcall

There is little to be said about the simple overcall itself, except to say that modern expert practice allows it to be made on stronger hands than previously, so that to double then bid a new suit tends to show a very strong hand.

A change of suit response to an overcall can be played as forcing, encouraging but non-forcing, or as a rescue. Of these, the last is very much out of fashion and rightly so.

The most flexible is the middle course, where a new suit is constructive but passable. In fact, a compromise is probably best, to play that a new suit at the one level or after a two-level overcall is forcing, but a two over one response is only constructive but passable.

Pre-emptive Raises

An immediate raise or jump raise of an overcall is best played as pre-emptive. The argument is that if your side has a trump fit then so have your opponents. The weaker you are the more reason there is to raise the level of the bidding as high as possible and as quickly as possible to make it tough for them to find their fit and level. Accordingly, after 1♣ – 1♠ – Pass/Dble – ?

	(i)	♠ K J 3	(ii)	♠ K J 6 3
		♡ 8 6 3		♡ 8 6
		♢ J 6 4 2		♢ J 6 4 2
		♣ 8 7 5		♣ 8 7 5

Non-vulnerable, hand (i) should raise to 2♠ and hand (ii) to 3♠. Vulnerable, both should raise but perhaps 2♠ is enough on (ii), at least against non-vulnerable opponents.

Unassuming Cuebids

If immediate raises of partner's suit are to be pre-emptive, then another way has to be found to make constructive raises. The most popular is the unassuming cuebid. All this means is that, where a bid of the opponents' suit was traditionally a game force, now it merely promises a high-card raise in partner's suit. A good idea is to raise to the level you are willing to go immediately, so a jump cuebid should also be a constructive raise. After 1♣ – 1♠ – Pass – ?

(iii)	♠ K J 2	(iv)	♠ K J 2
	♡ A 6 5 2		♡ A K 6 2
	◇ Q 8 4 3		◇ K 8 4 3
	♣ 10 6		♣ 10 6

(iii) should show a constructive raise to 2♠ by cuebidding 2♣, while (iv) should show a constructive raise to 3♠ by bidding 3♣. The precise strength required to make a constructive raise will vary slightly according to vulnerability and overcalling style.

A hand which is worth an old-fashioned game force can also start with a cuebid. To cuebid then bid a new suit or cuebid again shows such a hand.

2NT as a Raise

Some tournament pairs play a jump response of 2NT to an overcall as another kind of raise. How you share out the different bids between different hand-types is a matter for agreement, but one possibility is to play that the jump cuebid is very invitational and 2NT only mildly so, or perhaps that both are of similar overall strength but one shows four-card trump support and the other only three. The assumption is that a hand worth a natural 2NT response can always find a different bid and call 2NT on the next round. After a two-level overcall, however, this is not the case and 2NT should now retain its natural meaning.

Fit Jumps

A jump shift can be played as natural and forcing, the traditional meaning, while a double jump shift such as 4♣ opposite a 1♠ overcall is a Splinter – just as opposite an opening bid – or it can be played as a Fit Jump. The Fit Jump is a fairly new idea. It comes out of the principle that, when supporting partner in a competitive auction, it is best to do so as descriptively as possible to allow him to judge what to do next. A Fit Jump shows trump support for partner, a reasonable suit of your own, and the playing strength to go to the level at which you have bid. For example, after 1♡ – 1♠ – Pass/Dble:

(i)	♠ K 6 4 2	(ii)	♠ A J 4 2
	♡ 8 5		♡ A 5
	◇ A J 10 8 4		◇ A J 10 8 4
	♣ 7 3		♣ 7 3

Hand (i) is worth a raise to 3♠ so bids 3◇, showing the side suit as well. Hand (ii) is worth a raise to 4♠ so bids 4◇. In the event that the auction continues to be competitive, not only will partner know the strength of your hand, he will also be able to judge whether you have a fit or misfit in the side suits, thereby helping him to 'guess' right whether to pass, bid or double.

In principle, Fit Jumps are a good idea. But beware of misusing the bids, as the side suit does need to be of a reasonable quality.

Fit Non-jumps

Occasionally, it is possible to make the same kind of fit bid without jumping, usually because a previous pass has made it impossible for you to hold a hand worthy of a purely natural bid in a new suit.

For example:

West	North	East	South
1♣	Pass	1◇	1♠
3♣	3♡		

If North could not overcall 1♡ or 2♡ on the first round, how can he suddenly introduce a new suit at the three level? He must also have a spade fit, e.g:

```
♠ K J 6 4
♡ K Q J 3
◇ 7 3
♣ J 8 5
```

If you are going to bid 3♠, why not give partner more information by bidding 3♡ instead?

The Takeout Double

As with the overcall, there is little to be said about the takeout double. A double of an opening suit bid shows at least opening values and asks partner to tell you what suit he likes best (if any) and how strong he is.

While there is scope for personal style here, as in most things, a rough guide would be that after: 1♣ – Dble – Pass – ?

```
1◇/♡/♠  = 0-7 HCP
2◇/♡/♠  = 8-11 HCP
1NT     = 6-10 HCP
2NT     = 11-12 HCP
```

All of the above can be reduced slightly if a long suit is held. Stronger hands either bid game immediately if they know where they are going or cuebid the opponents' suit.

For example:

$$\spadesuit \; K J 6 2$$
$$\heartsuit \; K J 6 2$$
$$\diamondsuit \; 8 5$$
$$\clubsuit \; A J 3$$

Rather than guess to bid 4♡/♠ or 3NT, bid 2♣ and check to see if there really is a 4-4 major suit fit. If there is, you can bid that game, while in the unlikely event that partner has neither major you can bid 3NT.

Traditionally, the cuebid was forcing to game, allowing each player to bid his suits until a fit was found. Many tournament pairs allow the cuebid to be used on hands of only invitational strength upwards, saying it is forcing to suit agreement. So:

West	North	East	South
1♣	Dble	Pass	2♣
Pass	2♡	Pass	2♠

is forcing, because 2♠ is a new suit, but:

West	North	East	South
1♣	Dble	Pass	2♣
Pass	2♡	Pass	3♡

is non-forcing, because a suit has been agreed.

This allows, say, a 10 HCP hand with 4-4 in the majors, to get to the right trump suit, which a simple jump to 2♡/♠ might not achieve. A player with extra values must remember to bid game once a fit is found. This seems to be an improvement on traditional methods.

Intermediate Jump Overcalls

Traditionally, a jump overcall showed a strong hand with a good six-card suit. These hands come up quite rarely and can always be shown when they do by starting with a double then bidding or jumping in the suit. Intermediate jumps are not so strong, showing a sound opening bid with a decent six-card suit, the kind of hand where, if you started with a simple overcall, you might be tempted to bid a second time if the opportunity presented itself. Over 1♣, this would be a typical 2♡ overcall:

♠ A 5 3
♡ A Q 10 9 6 5
♢ K 4
♣ 7 3

From a constructive point of view, this is the best strength to show with a jump overcall, getting the hand off your chest in one go. It is also much more common than the old-style strong jump.

As with simple overcalls, an immediate raise can be at least semi-pre-emptive, constructive raises going via a cuebid. A change of suit should be played as forcing.

Weak Jump Overcalls

A big majority of the world's experts play jump overcalls as weak, or pre-emptive. Over 1♣, a typical non-vulnerable 2♡ bid might be:

♠ J 3
♡ K J 9 7 3 2
♢ 6 4 3
♣ 8 4

Vulnerable, you might like to have the ♡Q instead of the ♡2. In other words, a jump overcall shows a hand very similar to one which would have made the same bid as opener, had it had the chance.

The idea is that, even more than as dealer, when an opponent has opened the bidding, the hand rates to belong to your opponents if you have a long suit but relatively few high cards. Hence, you want to make life difficult for them and a pre-emptive jump may do just that.

Though many would argue that weak jumps are theoretically unsound, and the statistics at the very top level suggest that they actually lose points in the long run, most players have trouble handling them sufficiently often that they are definite point winners at normal tournament level.

You can respond as though partner had opened with a weak two or three bid. A raise is pre-emptive, a new suit natural and either forcing or merely constructive as you prefer, and a cuebid strong.

Opposite a two-level weak jump,. it makes sense to play 2NT as an artificial enquiry in the same way as opposite a weak two opening; you will rarely want to bid a natural and invitational 2NT, after all.

Incidentally, whatever range of jump overcalls you play in second position, in the pass-out seat a jump overcall should be intermediate. There is not much point in pre-empting when you could just pass the hand out, is there?

Two-suited Overcalls

There are several schemes of two-suited overcalls in existence, some showing both suits immediately, some being less precise. One thing they all have in common is that they should guarantee at least 5-5 in the two suits.

It is a good idea to have some way of showing a genuine two-suiter because such hands are often difficult to show in other ways. Virtually no strength of two-suiter should begin with a takeout double, as they are almost impossible to describe properly later. The alternative is to make a simple overcall and hope to get a second chance to show the other suit. That is O.K. with a good hand but some weaker hands are worth only one bid and risk the second suit being lost.

One quite common approach is to play the two-suited bids as either weak or strong, with a gap in the middle. So if 1♣ – 2♣ shows both majors, for example, it may be 8-12 HCP or 16+, or something similar, but not in the middle. This is quite a sound idea, though not essential, and is designed to help constructive bidding. Responder assumes the weak variety and bids accordingly. With the strong type, responder bids again freely. When holding the intermediate range, you start with a simple overcall but then bid your second suit on the next round unless either you have already found a fit or the auction has reached a very high level.

The Unusual No Trump

The one two-suited overcall which is played by almost all duplicate players is the Unusual No Trump, in which a 2NT overcall shows the lowest two unbid suits (a less popular variant has it showing both minors over a major and both majors over a minor). In response, partner usually bids to the level he thinks he is worth in his preferred suit.

In fourth position, after one of a suit has been passed round, 2NT should be played as natural, around 19-21 balanced, as otherwise it is too difficult to fit in all the different balanced ranges.

The Unusual No Trump overcall can also occur in other situations where it is impossible for it to be natural, for example:

West	North	East	South
Pass	Pass	Pass	1♡
1NT			

Clearly the overcaller cannot have a strong no-trump hand. More likely he is something like 5-4 in the minors, strong enough to compete but not sufficiently shapely to overcall 2NT.

Ghestem

In Ghestem, both suits are shown immediately.

2NT   = The lowest two unbid suits
Cuebid = The two extreme unbid suits
3♣   = The highest two unbid suits

Over a 1♣ opening bid, there are two variations; in both, 3♣ shows spades and diamonds, while either 2♣ or 2♢ can show the majors, with 2♣ being natural when not needed as a two-suiter.

Showing both suits immediately is a good idea, as it means that you cannot be pre-empted out of ever finding a fit in the second suit if it is not defined. Unfortunately, many players seem to have memory problems with Ghestem. The 3♣ overcall in particular causes more problems for Appeals Committees in tournament bridge than any other convention.

Apart from memory problems, the only other price of playing this method is the loss of a natural 3♣ overcall – the cuebid and 2NT overcalls are a negligible loss.

Roman Jump Overcalls

This scheme also shows both suits immediately, except with strong hands. A jump overcall shows the bid suit plus the next higher ranking unbid suit, for example, after a 1♢ opening:

2♡ = Hearts and spades
2♠ = Spades and clubs
3♣ = Clubs and hearts

All these bids are limited in strength and partner usually bids his preferred suit at the level he wishes to play.

A 2NT overcall shows a strong two-suiter in any two of the unbid suits. Responder should bid the cheapest unbid suit in response. Now it gets slightly complicated. If the overcaller now bids 3NT, he shows that he has the other two suits and wants partner to choose one at the four level. If he bids a suit, he shows that suit plus the one responder was forced to bid, and if he bids a suit at the three level, responder is allowed to pass with a very poor hand. For example, after 1♢ – 2NT – Pass – 3♣ (lowest unbid suit):

3♡ = Hearts and clubs, non-forcing
3♠ = Spades and clubs, non-forcing
3NT = Hearts and spades, game-forcing
4♡ = Hearts and clubs, game-forcing
4♠ = Spades and clubs, game-forcing

Showing both suits immediately is a good idea, and also splitting big hands from ordinary two-suiters is useful, but the loss of all those natural jump overcalls is a big price to pay. The obvious thing to do is to play a cuebid as an unspecified jump overcall to partially fill the gap, but it is much harder to bid effectively opposite this than opposite a natural jump.

Michaels Cuebids

Michaels Cuebids do not always specify both suits. 2NT is always the lowest two unbid suits, while a cuebid of a minor shows both majors. So far so good, but there is no way of showing, say, spades and diamonds over a 1♣ opening. And a cuebid in a major shows the other major plus an unspecified minor. All combinations are catered for, but if the third player raises his partner's suit, you may never discover which minor is held by the overcaller.

Responses to the overcalls are as normal where both suits have been shown. After 1♠ – 2♠ – Pass –? and 1♡ – 2♡ – Pass – ?, responder who does not have support for the promised major needs to find out which minor his partner holds.

The simple scheme is that 2NT enquires and the overcaller shows his suit at the three level with a weak hand and jumps with the strong version. If responder instead bids three of a minor, that is natural and forcing.

The other possibility is to play a three of a minor response as being for correction, i.e. the overcaller passes or raises with the suit bid, converts to the other minor with that suit. This makes it impossible for responder to introduce the fourth suit, but allows him to show his enthusiasm for competing in one of the overcaller's suits.

For example, after 1♡ – 2♡ – Pass/Dble – ?:

2NT   = Weak or strong, please bid your minor. Only compete further
        if strong, otherwise, leave it to me.
3♣/◇ = Intermediate strength and support for both minors. Partner is
        invited to compete further if they bid on.

That last is a useful improvement. Michaels does not take away any natural overcalls, but its failure to show all possible combinations clearly is a serious weakness. One other positive feature is that major two-suiters, the most important of all, are shown by bidding two of a minor, so that responder can choose either suit at the two level. Some players take advantage of this by allowing a major two-suiter to be only 5-4, but I am against this as it makes it much harder for partner to bid effectively.

The Jump Cuebid

A jump cuebid, such as $1\heartsuit - 3\heartsuit$, is a pretty useless bid in a natural sense. A use has been found, however – to ask partner to bid 3NT if he has the suit stopped. Typically, the user will have a long running suit and at least one of the other two suits stopped. For example, over a $1\heartsuit$ opening:

	(i)		(ii)
	♠ K 7		♠ A Q
	♡ 6 3		♡ 7
	◇ A K Q 10 9 7 5		◇ A K Q J 8 7 4
	♣ A 3		♣ 8 6 3

Either of these hands would bid $3\heartsuit$, as indeed might some slightly weaker examples. It is true that (ii) is also wide open in clubs, but it is a reasonable gamble to hope that a heart stopper is all you need for 3NT.

In response, partner normally bids 3NT with the desired stopper. Failing that, he may bid a long suit at the three level or 4♣, allowing partner to pass or correct to his actual suit. With no stopper but enough to play game in partner's suit, responder can cuebid in return.

Defences to One No Trump

Standard methods are to play double for penalties, showing a hand which is better than the opener's, 2NT as any strong two-suiter, and other bids as natural. This leaves far too many hands with which you would like to bid but have no suit strong enough to overcall so have to pass. Accordingly, a whole host of artificial defences have been invented to show various two- and three-suited hand-types, and allowing competition on almost any hand with some high card strength plus an unbalanced distribution.

As always, when considering taking on a new convention, it is necessary to look at the cost of the new method. Apart from more complex considerations such as giving away valuable information to an opponent who may eventually become declarer, the main cost is the loss of those natural bids which are used in an artificial sense. Most defences to 1NT use 2♣ and 2◇ as artificial bids. This means that some single-suiters can no longer be shown but these are in the minors which are relatively less important as, even when you hold a suitable hand, you are frequently outbid in a major anyway. In return, you gain the ability to show many other hands and the price is unquestionably worth paying. Note that you cannot bid 2♣ as a two-way bid, either clubs or artificial. Firstly, the bridge authorities frown on such methods, whereby 2♣ followed by 3♣ means you had clubs all along; secondly, it makes constructive bidding very difficult for responder.

Most defences are based on showing two-suiters, usually but not always at least 5-4, while a few are based on three-suiters. As genuine three-suiters are comparatively rare and semi-three-suiters, such as 5-4-3-1, can be treated as two-suiters, I favour showing two-suiters on frequency grounds – plus, two-suiters tend to have greater playing strength and so are safer hands with which to compete.

There is a good case for playing a double as artificial, showing some non-penalty hand-type, at least against a strong no-trump opening when it will be rare to hold a penalty double. In Britain, the bridge authorities do not permit this in many open events, reserving it for competitions likely to attract only more regular tournament players. When defending against a weak no-trump, it is less clear whether the loss of the penalty double is justifiable, though one or two of the newer defences on the market use double conventionally, again largely on frequency grounds.

What is clear is that you need to be able to come into the auction as often as possible and to be able to show single-suiters based on a major and two-suiters including one or more major suits. Any defence which does not permit this is flawed.

Finally, whatever basic defence you choose, you can usually add an artificial meaning for a 2NT overcall, either the traditional strong two-suiter or perhaps to show both minors. And you must decide what a jump overcall means. Traditionally, this showed a hand too strong for a simple overcall. Nowadays, more and more people are playing it as pre-emptive. The latter treatment can cause serious problems for your opponents, at least if used in second position (there is less point in fourth seat after they have already tried to pass out 1NT), but it means that all reasonable hands with a long minor must remain silent on the first round and hope to get a second chance – 2♣/◇ is artificial, 3♣/◇ is weak.

ANTI
Double = Natural
2♣   = Diamonds OR both majors
2◇   = Hearts OR spades and a minor
2♡   = Hearts and a minor
2♠   = Spades
2NT   = Both minors

In response to 2♣/◇/♡, 2NT is an artificial enquiry, normally based on a good hand. Over 2♣, 2◇ is to play opposite diamonds, the overcaller correcting to 2♡ with both majors. 2♡/♠ is to play opposite the majors but willing to play in at least 3◇ opposite diamonds. Over 2◇, 2♡ is to play opposite hearts, the overcaller correcting to 2♠ with spades and a minor. 2♠ is to play opposite spades but shows a willingness to play in at least 3♡ opposite hearts.

Aspro

2♣ = Hearts and another suit
2♢ = Spades and a minor

Other calls are natural.

Responder can bid the next suit up as a non-forcing relay, to ask for the second suit. The overcaller will pass if this is his second suit, bid the anchor suit with five, or bid the second suit if that is of five cards. Usually, however, responder will bid the anchor suit when holding three- or more- card support and no interest in game. By agreement, either 2NT or a raise of the artificial overcall can be used as a forcing enquiry with a strong hand. While the latter is the more popular version, 2NT leaves more space and allows greater accuracy so is recommended

Astro

2♣ = Hearts and a minor
2♢ = Spades and another

Responses are as in Aspro.

Asptro

2♣ = Hearts and another
2♢ = Spades and another

This is a combination of Aspro and Astro, the difference being that with both majors there is a choice of overcalls. When holding both majors you may, by agreement, anchor to the longer or shorter. It looks more natural to anchor to the longer suit, but there is a marginal advantage in doing it the other way round, meaning that you get to the better major suit fit slightly more often.

2NT would be the forcing response opposite either overcall. There seems to be no generally agreed scheme of responses to this. A matter for a serious partnership to discuss.

Brozel

Double	=	Any one-suiter
2♣	=	Hearts and clubs
2♢	=	Hearts and diamonds
2♡	=	Hearts and spades
2♠	=	Spades and a minor
2NT	=	Both minors
3 any	=	Three-suiter, short in the bid suit

Opposite a double, a good hand can pass for penalties, the definition of good depending on partner's style, just how weak he might be to double with his single-suiter. If responder does not wish to defend 1NT doubled, he bids 2♣. The doubler now passes or bids his suit.

Where both suits are shown immediately, a 2NT response would be natural and invitational. The forcing enquiry should be a bid of the unbid minor, 3♣ where both are unbid.

Most of the time, both suits are shown immediately with a two-suiter, which is good news, as is the ability to show three-suiters, though they must be quite strong to justify driving to the three-level. There is no way for a weakish responder to discover which of partner's suits is the longer, as he often can if using one of the Astro family, and the penalty double is lost. A really big balanced hand can start by doubling, then bid 2NT when partner runs to 2♣. This at least gets the hand-type across, but partner will never be strong enough to play for penalties. A flat 17-count, for example, just has to pass initially – hardly ideal.

Cansino

2♣ = Three-suited with at least tolerance for clubs
2♦ = Both majors

In response to 2♣, 2NT is a forcing enquiry, with common-sense responses. Opposite a 2♦ bid, 2NT is natural and 3♣ the enquiry.

Cansino was one of the earlier defences to 1NT and is losing its popularity nowadays. Its biggest single weakness is that major-minor two-suiters are completely uncatered for.

Michael Cappelletti

When he is not devising bridge conventions, Michael Cappelletti is likely to be found in a court of law, as he is an attorney with the United States Department of Justice.

Apart from his skill at bridge – he was a member of the team that took third place in the 1974 World Mixed Teams Championship – he is considered to be one of the world's foremost authorities on Omaha Poker, writing a regular column for *The Card Player* magazine since 1989. His convention is described in detail in Capelletti over No-Trump.

Cappelletti

2♣ = Any one-suiter
2♦ = Both majors
2♡ = Hearts and a minor
2♠ = Spades and a minor
2NT = Both minors or a strong major-minor two-suiter

The overcalls are usually limited to around 14 HCP. Stronger hands usually start with a double if one-suited or big and balanced, or bid 2NT if a major-minor two-suiter. Opposite 2NT, partner assumes a moderate minor two-suiter until proven otherwise. Obviously, a subsequent bid of a major by the 2NT bidder shows the strong type.

Opposite 2♦, 2NT is natural and invitational, 3♣ an enquiry. Opposite 2♡/♠, 2NT asks for the minor. It is possible here to play that 2NT is always constructive and that 3♣/♦ is for correction with a poor hand.

DONT

Double = Any one-suiter
2♣ = Clubs and any other suit
2♦ = Diamonds and a major
2♡ = Both majors
2♠ = Spades (weaker than double then 2♠)

This is one of the new generation of defences. It is based on the premise that the important thing is to interfere over a 1NT opening; getting to game or the highest scoring partscore being less important. Unlike other defences, it is not orientated towards the majors; all suits are deemed to be equally important and all that matters is finding a playable fit. It is a particularly attractive method against a strong no-trump, where bidding game your way is much less likely, as is a fruitful penalty double.

Opposite the double, responder normally bids 2♣, the doubler passing or correcting to his suit. Opposite the two-suited overcalls, responder passes with a fit or bids his lowest playable suit and the overcaller then passes or bids his suit if he can do so at the two-level. Responder should always consider the possibility that partner does not have the second suit he would like.

For example, opposite a 2♦ overcall (diamonds and a major), it is fine for a 4-3-3-3 hand to bid 2♡, looking to play in partner's major, but with 1-4-3-5 it is wiser to pass 2♦ – partner will surely have spades, not hearts.

As the whole philosophy of DONT is to disturb 1NT, users will tend to be willing to bid on quite weak hands so responder should not punish them by looking for game unless holding an exceptional hand himself. Also, most two-suited defences assume at least 5-4 in the two suits; while DONT

Alvin Landy

Like many bridge players, Alvin Landy was a lawyer by profession, collecting his degree in 1927. After serving in World War II he joined the ACBL as a tournament director, and rapidly climbed the ladder, becoming the league's business manager and chief executive. He played a key role in the creation of the ACBL Charity Foundation. Landy's outstanding administrative qualities were recognised by the WBF – he served as one of their officers when that organisation was formed.

also prefers that sort of shape, because all combinations can be shown at the two-level, DONT allows 4-4 hands to bid a little more frequently when the vulnerability makes it seem appropriate.

Landy

Perhaps the simplest of all conventional defences to 1NT. All bids are natural except that a 2♣ overcall promises both majors. In response, 3♣ is the forcing enquiry while 2◇ shows equal length in the majors and asks the 2♣ bidder to choose. Other bids are natural and, other than 2♡/♠, constructive.

Landy is simple and easy to remember and it is certainly more useful to be able to show both majors than to bid a natural 2♣. There are too many hand-types which cannot be shown, however, and while it is a good choice for your first conventional defence to give you a feel for such things, a regular tournament pair will want something a little more complex.

Lionel

Double = 11+, Spades and another, at least 4-4
2♣   = 11+, Hearts and clubs, at least 4-4
2◇   = 11+, Hearts and diamonds, at least 4-4
2♡/♠ = Natural

Another of the new generation of defences. Opposite the double, pass with 10+ HCP or bid 2♣ as a non-forcing relay – partner passes or bids his second suit. You can play all other bids as natural, but the official version has 3♠ as pre-emptive, 2NT as an invitational spade raise with no shortage, and three of a suit as a spade raise with shortage in the bid suit.

Opposite 2♣ / ◇, all bids are natural, invitational if 2NT or a jump.

You lose the penalty double of 1NT, but gain by being able to defend 1NT doubled more often when the strength is divided between your two hands. Again, the philosophy is to disturb 1NT and compete the partscore effectively. As with DONT, Lionel allows you to play two of a minor where most two-suited defences, geared to the majors, make this virtually impossible. As with all methods which show both suits immediately, you are well placed in competition but weak responding hands will not be able to discover which five-card suit, if any, is held. Overall, Lionel is quite promising, however.

Ripstra

An old and becoming relatively unpopular, defence to 1NT. It is similar to Landy in that it concentrates on the majors. This time, however, both 2♣ and 2◇ guarantee at least 4-4 in the majors, with the better minor being bid. In response, 2NT is an enquiry and a raise of the minor is natural and constructive.

Ripstra works well on three-suited hands with both majors but less well than Landy on two-suiters when you have to show an anchor minor on a doubleton – as this may be passed, it is not an attractive prospect. Also, two- and three-suiters with only one major are not catered for.

Wallis

2♣	=	Major-minor two-suiter
2◇	=	Both majors
2♡/♠ =		Natural
2NT	=	Both minors

In response to 2♣, 2NT should be the enquiry as you could never know that you wanted to play there when not knowing partner's suits. Over 2◇, however, 3♣ is best used as the enquiry and 2NT as natural and invitational. It is possible to play 3♣ / ◇ responses to 2◇ as natural and constructive; an alternative is for 3♡ / ♠ to be pre-emptive and 3♣ / ◇ to be invitational raises in hearts/spades respectively.

Wallis is difficult to defend against because the 2♣ overcall does not specify any suits. It is also difficult to play, for the same reason. In response to 2♣, new suit bids are for correction, i.e. only to play if you have hit one of the overcaller's suits. Responder will often have quite awkward guesses to make.

If you like to know where you are in the auction you will not like Wallis; if you like to live on your wits and see everyone at the table having problems, you may enjoy it. Because there is no anchor suit, it is not permitted in many domestic events.

Coping With Intervention

Whatever defence you choose to play, it is important to know what you are doing if the opponents compete, in particular with a double. The main thing is to be on the same wavelength, but here is a scheme for use with any of those methods where both suits are not defined immediately by the overcall.

For example, 1NT – 2♣ (hearts and another) – Double – ?

Pass	=	To play opposite clubs
2♢	=	Natural, a long diamond suit
2♡	=	Support
2♠	=	Natural, a long spade suit
Redouble	=	Get us out of here

The important features here are the meanings of pass and redouble. If you are clear on these, then everything else falls into place without risk of any misunderstanding.

Defences to a Strong Two Club Opening

Any defence to a strong one club opening can also be used against a strong two club opening, however, you are starting a level higher and any two-suited bid which commits your side to the three level really should promise at least 5-5 in the two suits and some playing strength. The basic aim is still, however, destructive, an attempt to make life difficult for the opposition.

My own view would be that any defence which obliges you to go to the three level to show a single-suited hand is a poor choice as many hands are worth a simple overcall at the two level but not a jump to three. So I am against such as Truscott, but quite happy, for example, with any of the Crash variants.

Defences to Pre-empts
DEFENCES TO WEAK TWO BIDS

Standard methods are to simply treat weak two openings as though they were one openings. In other words, all overcalls are natural and double is for takeout. The problem with this is that the response to the double takes you uncomfortably close to the game level, leaving no room to make an invitational bid. After all, responder must bid even with nothing, so how is the doubler to know whether that is the case or whether his partner actually has eight or nine points and was very happy to be asked to bid?

Of the alternatives described below, two are designed to get around precisely this problem.

2NT for Takeout

This leaves double available to penalise the opposition, while other bids are natural. It has the disadvantages of making strong no-trump types difficult to show, getting no-trump contracts played the wrong way up, and making it impossible to play in a two-level contract. It also does nothing to resolve the problem of responder's bids having such a wide range. All you get in return, is the ability to make penalty doubles; the price is too high.

Hackett

In Hackett, 2NT is natural, around 16-18 HCP, double is penalty, and there are two takeout bids – 3♣ on moderate hands up to about 16 HCP, 3♦ with stronger hands. By splitting the takeout bids into two ranges, many of the awkward decisions can be resolved, it becoming responder's responsibility to decide whether game is likely, given partner's range.

Say the auction begins 2♡ – Dble – Pass – 2♠ – Pass – ? Playing takeout doubles, you would be tempted to raise to 3♠ with:

> ♠ A Q 8 3
> ♡ 8
> ◇ K Q J 5
> ♣ K Q 4 2

If, however, you had already shown 17+ by bidding 3◇ for takeout, you could pass 2♠, safe in the knowledge that partner will have already played you for this much.

Paul Hackett

Paul Hackett is the father of the well known Hackett twins, but is an outstanding player in his own right, having represented both England and Great Britain with distinction. Having tried to set up a worldwide tournament circuit that failed for lack of finance, he turned to professional playing, and with the aid of his sons has captured many International events.

This goes some way towards solving an awkward problem and also allows you to penalise an opponent who steps out of line. Against that, two natural bids are lost, and again final contracts of 2♠, 2NT and perhaps 3♣ are made unplayable. Also, responder cannot convert the takeout bid and play for penalties as he can when facing a takeout double. All in all, a step in the right direction but not good enough.

Takeout Doubles with Lebensohl

The Lebensohl convention was first invented to solve a problem when the opposition bid over your partner's 1NT opening. Here, the same principle of an artificial 2NT bid, allows responder to divide his hands into two ranges, one very weak, the other of invitational strength. It works like this:

2♡ – Dble – Pass – ?

2♠	= 4+spades, 0-6 HCP
2NT	= Artificial relay
3♣/◇	= 4+cards, 7-10 HCP
3♡	= Cuebid – no heart stopper, not four spades
3♠	= 7-10 HCP with good spades
3NT/4any	= Natural, game force

2♠ – Dble – Pass – ?

2NT	= Artificial relay
3♣/◇/♡	= Natural, 7-10 HCP
3♠	= Cuebid – no spade stopper, not four hearts
3NT/4any	= Natural, game force

Unless very strong, i.e. interested in game even opposite 0-6 HCP, the doubler bids 3♣ over the artificial 2NT response, enabling responder to show his hand-type. Responder rebids:

Pass	= 0-6 with clubs
3◇	= 0-6 with diamonds
3NT	= Game values, stopper and four cards in other major
Cuebid	= Game values, no stopper but four cards in other major

After a 2♠ opening, 3♡ = 0-6 with hearts
After a 2♡ opening, 3♠ = 7-10 with spades but scattered values

This scheme is a good deal more complicated, particularly because of the various 3NT and cuebids, but it does go a long way towards solving the basic problem and you could play it without the cuebids etc if you preferred. There will still be awkward combinations of ranges, but they will be less common than under any other scheme. Also, no natural bids are lost, the two prices being the loss of the penalty double and the inability to play in 2NT after a takeout double.

Some form of Takeout Doubles with Lebensohl is played by the big majority of good players and is undoubtedly superior to anything else in current use.

Leaping Michaels

The idea of Leaping Michaels is that a 4♣ or 4◊ overcall of a weak two bid is a pretty rare animal in a natural sense – the bidder will rarely be prepared to go past 3NT if holding a good hand based on a long minor suit. Accordingly, to use these overcalls in an artificial sense is almost cost free and the idea is that they should be reasonable hands with at least 5-5 in the bid minor plus the unbid major, thereby allowing an awkward hand-type to be shown in one bid.

This makes a lot of sense. The two-suiters are not that common, but they are tough to show otherwise. The only other bid which might be used to show such a two-suiter is an immediate cuebid. If playing Leaping Michaels, the cuebid can be reserved for hands that want to ask partner to bid 3NT with a stopper, thereby solving another otherwise unbiddable hand-type.

DEFENCES TO THE MULTI 2◊

Though a Multi 2◊ opening often includes at least one strong option, the vast majority of the time it will be based on a weak two bid in a major. Unfortunately, you cannot simply defend as though it really is a weak two bid as you don't know which suit the opener has. Most defences to the Multi make it a very high priority to try to tell partner which suit you think the opener holds.

A very simple defence would be to play that, in both second and fourth seats, double is takeout of hearts and 2NT takeout of spades, leaving all other bids as natural. This does not leave room for responder to make an invitational bid opposite the 2NT takeout, and it means that a natural 2NT overcall must pass first time around and bid at its second opportunity. Perhaps more serious is that it does not cater for balanced hands in the 12-15 HCP range, and if two such hands face each other it may be difficult to have an intelligent auction.

It would also be possible to invert the meanings of double and 2NT; indeed, that is what is done in the Reese-Dormer defence to the Multi, which is otherwise natural.

Dixon

In second seat:

2♡	= Non-forcing takeout of a weak 2♠ opener
2♠	= Non-forcing takeout of a weak 2♡ opener
2NT	= 16-19 balanced

Double = 13-15 balanced or any strong hand which can handle the
         subsequent auction
Others = Natural and non-forcing

After passing, a double is penalty orientated and suit bids are natural but weaker than if made immediately. A cuebid is the strong takeout and 2NT shows a minor two-suiter.

Partner will assume that an initial double shows 13-15 balanced until proven otherwise. To double and then bid again opposite a passed partner would show a strong hand, too good for an initial overcall, with double then double again showing 20+ (semi-)balanced.

In fourth seat:

2♠   = Non-forcing takeout of a weak 2♡ opener
2NT   = 16-19 balanced
Double = 13-15 balanced or including the bid suit
Others = Natural and non-forcing

After passing, a double is for takeout and bids are natural but limited.

This scheme caters to those awkward moderate balanced hands which might otherwise be shut out of the auction. It leaves room for invitational bids in either major opposite the takeout bids, and it tells partner immediately which suit opener is likely to hold. Indeed, I would suggest that it is best to assume that opener has the unbid major after a takeout bid, allowing you to use a bid of that suit as a cuebid to allow strong hands to be developed intelligently.

But, though schemes of this type were very popular at one time, their big disadvantage is that they take away two very important natural bids, overcalls of 2♡ and 2♠. For me, that is too high a price to pay.

Takeout Doubles With Lebensohl

The most popular method among serious tournament players at the moment is to play that all overcalls are natural and three-suited hands with a shortage in one major pass on the first round then double for takeout after the opener has unwound and his suit is known. So:

(i)	2♢	Pass	2♡/♠	Dble
(ii)	2♢	Pass	2♡/♠	Pass
	Pass/2♠	Dble		
(iii)	2♢	Pass	2♡/♠	Pass
	Pass/2♠	Pass	Pass	Dble

Double is for takeout in all of these sequences.

Effectively, you are defending exactly as if the opening had been a natural weak two bid. This allows responder to the double to use Lebensohl, as discussed above under Defences to Weak Two Bids, to show his strength and hand-type.

An immediate double of 2◇ shows the balanced 13-15 type or a big hand, as in Dixon.

Pass followed by 2NT is sometimes played as showing both minors and sometimes as a natural bid based on a hand with which you intended to make a takeout double had opener shown the other major. This is a matter for partnership agreement. My guess is that the minor two-suiter will be more frequent but that on those rare occasions where you do hold the other hand-type you will be completely stuck if you do not have a natural 2NT bid available.

Reverse Leaping Michaels

Just as Leaping Michaels can be played to show two-suiters after the opposition have opened with a natural weak two bid, so Reverse Leaping Michaels can be used over a Multi. If playing this way, a four-of-a-minor overcall shows at least 5-5 in the bid minor plus an unspecified major.

The method obviously does not work as well as over a natural weak two as the overcaller's major suit is not known. It may be better to simply pass on the first round then use Leaping Michaels after opener has said which suit he holds.

DEFENCES TO WEAK THREE BIDS

Even more than weak two bids, three-level pre-empts cause problems for the opposition – that is why people play them. There is no longer room for game invitational sequences opposite a takeout bid and the whole thing becomes very difficult.

The important thing is to develop a philosophy – a set of guidelines to keep to whenever an awkward situation arises. Firstly, it is necessary to accept that the pre-empt will sometimes do its job and we will be completely fixed; we will suspect that we can make something but have no intelligent way to find out. In other words, we will be left guessing. When this happens, we should not strive for perfection on every deal, rather, we should attempt always to get a sensible result. Rather than strive for the best possible result, accept the best result practicably possible.

Secondly, try to take the pressure off partner. Any bid will inevitably cover quite a wide range of hands, so try not to leave him guessing whether his meagre values are just what you need for game; better to just bash game if you need only a little help from partner.

Thirdly, remember that the pre-empt suggests a distributional hand and therefore the possibility of bad breaks. If in doubt, take a cautious view.

And, finally, don't be too worried about trying to penalise the pre-emptor; concentrate on getting to your own best contract and only take those penalties that come fairly easily within that approach. If you instead gear your bidding to collecting penalties, it will be much tougher to bid your own hands constructively when that is necessary.

As far as bidding methods are concerned, there are a whole host of defences available. In deciding which one to use, you should consider which hand-types you need to be able to show and therefore which bids you need in a natural sense. Then you can decide what bid(s) remains for use as your takeout bid.

I would say that you need to be able to bid 3NT as an attempt to play there, otherwise balanced hands and hands with a long minor suit with good values and a stopper in the enemy suit become unmanageable. Also, simple and jump bids in an unbid major are needed in a natural sense. Relatively speaking, unbid minors are less important, though you would like to be able to show them in an ideal world. And, of course, you must have a takeout bid, to ask partner to choose a trump suit.

Takeout Doubles

The overwhelming choice of the expert community is the simple takeout double, just as over a one-level opening. It has the merit of simplicity; it allows all other bids to retain their natural meaning; and it is far and away the most flexible method.

Its only drawback is, of course, that it prevents you from doubling for penalties. In fact, though that may seem a serious flaw, the takeout double picks up a significant number of penalties which a penalty double could not get, so the overall cost is lower than might be imagined.

Flexibility is a huge benefit. Compare a takeout double of a 3♦ opening with a 4♣ (Lower Minor) takeout bid. In response, partner can bid 3♥, 3♠, 3NT or Pass for penalties, none of which options are available opposite the 4♣ takeout bid. Plus, when you do jump to game, partner knows that you actually have something and can make an intelligent decision as to whether to look for slam – if you respond 4♥ to a 4♣ takeout bid, this becomes much more of a guessing game.

When responding to a takeout double, the scheme is pretty much the same as if responding to a double of one of a suit. Responder bids his preferred suit as cheaply as possible with a weak hand and forces to game with some useful values. The general rule is to imagine that partner has assumed about 7/8HCPs in your hand and only bid game if you have something above that. This allows the takeout double to be made on hands which cannot underwrite a contract at this level but which have sufficient strength that passing looks even more likely to produce a bad result.

As usual, once you decide that your hand is worth a game bid, you may simply bid the suit of your choice at game level or, if unsure which game will be best, can cuebid the opponents' suit.

There has been one important change in responding to takeout doubles at this level in recent years and that relates to the type of hand which passes the double for penalties. Traditionally, you only passed a takeout double if you held a strong trump holding. Total Trick Theory suggests that trump strength is not essential, mere length being sufficient. Take these hands:

(a) ♠ 10 8 6 4   (b) ♠ A 8 5 3
     ♡ A 6 3   ♡ K 6 3
     ◇ K 8 4   ◇ J 8 4 2
     ♣ J 6 2   ♣ K 4

When partner makes a takeout double of a 3♠ opening, the suggestion is that both these hands should pass. With (a), you have no reason to imagine that you can make any contract as, though you have some high card values, your side has no trump fit and will struggle at the four level. Note that, even if you have an eight-card fit, you may well not find it even if you do bid. Meanwhile, you can hope that you have sufficient high-card strength to defeat 3♠. If 3♠ doubled makes once in a while, that will be a reasonable price to pay for all the other times when bidding would have turned a plus score into a minus.

With hand (b), you have sufficient strength to think that you might make game. Still, however, you have no great trump fit so the game you will choose is 3NT. With no long suit and the possibility of bad breaks, it may be better in the long run to settle for the safe plus score on defence. You might take the vulnerability into account this time, gambling on 3NT when vulnerable against not, passing when they are vulnerable against not, and having a close decision at equal vulnerability.

Whether strong or weak, the current theory is that balanced hands should pass the takeout double far more readily than was previously believed. Clearly, this option only becomes available if your takeout bid is Double.

Responding to an Overcall

When partner makes a natural overcall, you can assume him to have a sound opening bid with a good five- or six-card suit. As when responding to a takeout double, you should discount the first 7HCPs or so in your hand and only consider raising to game with extra values. For example, after $3\diamond$ –$3\spadesuit$ – Pass – ?

(a) ♠ Q 6 3
     ♡ A 8 4 2
     ◇ 7 3
     ♣ Q 6 4 2

(b) ♠ J 8 5
     ♡ A 8 5 3
     ◇ Q 6
     ♣ Q 8 5 4

Both these hands are borderline raises to 4♠. You would probably just bid 4♠ with either of them but should not be at all surprised to see partner go down. Hand (b) in particular, with a potentially wasted queen, might well pass at matchpoint scoring, where there is less of a premium on bidding thin games.

The position becomes worse when you do not have support for partner. After $3\diamond$ – $3\spadesuit$ – Pass – ?

(c) ♠ J 6
     ♡ K J 7 4
     ◇ Q J 5 2
     ♣ J 9 8 6

Hand (c) is not worth a 3NT bid as it has so little to spare, no aces, and no real support for partner, better to pass.

The General Cuebid
Traditionally, the sequence: $3\diamond$ – $3\spadesuit$ –Pass – $4\diamond$, showed spade support, slam interest and a diamond control. A relatively recent innovation is to play the cuebid as showing spade support and slam interest but saying nothing about diamond control. Clearly, this comes up much more frequently and, because all slam tries start with the general cuebid, it means that there is no confusion about the meaning of a response in a new suit, in this case 4♣ or 4♡; these must now be natural.

Responding to a 3NT Overcall
A 3NT overcall can be a balanced 16HCPs, or a much stronger balanced hand; it can also be based on a long suit, again with a wide range of possible strengths. Natural methods are quite inadequate opposite such an overcall, particularly when slam is possible. A simple scheme is as follows:

After 3♠ –3NT – Pass – ?

4♣   = An artificial enquiry
4◇   = Demands 4♡ which responder will either pass or bid 4♠ to play
4♡/♠ = Non-forcing slam try with a long major

In response to 4♣, the overcaller shows his strength and hand-type as follows:

Harry Fishbein

Harry J Fishbein could always be recognised at the table, as he wore a beret, which rapidly became his trademark. He was President of the Mayfair Club and the treasurer of the ACBL from 1952 to 1966. He represented the USA in World Championship play both as a player and a captain.

4 of a suit	= Minimum with a long suit
4NT	= 16-18 balanced
5 of a suit	= Good hand with a long suit
5NT	= 19-21 balanced
6 of a suit	= Very good hand with a long suit
6NT	= 22+ balanced

Your definition of a good or very good hand will depend on personal style, while you may also wish to slightly alter the point ranges suggested for the various balanced hands.

Fishbein

In Fishbein, 3NT is natural and double is for penalties, the takeout bid being a bid of the next suit up, i.e. $3\clubsuit - 3\diamondsuit$; $3\diamondsuit - 3\heartsuit$; $3\heartsuit - 3\spadesuit$; $3\spadesuit - 4\clubsuit$ are all for takeout.

In the original version, the takeout bid was a one-round force and could be made on a two-suiter without the bid suit on occasion. This had the obvious disadvantage of getting the partnership too high on limited values and most players now play that the takeout bid is passable.

Fishbein is fairly simple to play but $3\diamondsuit - 3\heartsuit$ and $3\heartsuit - 3\spadesuit$ are valuable bids to lose in a natural sense, while $3\spadesuit - 4\clubsuit$ goes past 3NT. Also, while you can make penalty doubles, you cannot pass the takeout bid to convert it for penalties as you can when playing takeout doubles. Overall, the price is too high for what you get in return.

Lower Minor

As the name suggests, the takeout bid here is a bid of the lower unbid minor, $3\diamondsuit$ over $3\clubsuit$ and $4\clubsuit$ over anything else. Other bids are natural and double is penalty.

This is an improvement on Fishbein in that 4♣ is less needed in a natural sense than is three of a major, but it pushes the bidding to the four level far too often, making it impossible to play in three of a major or 3NT and also losing definition when responder bids four of a major – is he doing so because he has some useful values and expects to make his contract or merely because he was obliged to bid something? How is the 4♣ bidder to know when to bid on in search of slam and when not?

Foxu

This combines Fishbein and Takeout Doubles. In second position, Double is penalty and the next suit up is the takeout bid. In fourth position, Double is for Takeout.

I see precious little merit in this combination. One thing which is pretty clear is that double should have the same meaning in both positions. In Foxu, you can get a penalty when second seat has the trumps, either by his doubling or passing and waiting for partner's takeout double. If fourth seat has the trumps, nobody can double.

Film

This time, we are combining Fishbein and Lower Minor. Over 3♣, 3♢ is for takeout and over 3♠ the bid is 4♣, just as in either Fishbein or Lower Minor. The variation comes when defending against the red suits. 3♢ – 3♡ and 3♡ – 3♠ are both for takeout but promise four cards in the bid suit, while 4♣ is also for takeout but denies four cards in the next suit. Double is for penalties.

This gets over the problem faced by a weak responding hand which would like to pass the Fishbein bid but is unsure whether partner has any support for the suit, but it takes two natural bids away instead of one and, as with all these passable takeout bids, leaves the player making the takeout bid with no way of bidding a really strong takeout hand where he would be unhappy to hear his bid passed out.

Optional Double

Very simply, a double by either player shows a good opening hand with, in principle, tolerance for all the unbid suits plus some strength in opener's suit. It is ideally a fairly balanced hand and invites partner to pass if he is also balanced and otherwise to bid.

Played on its own, it has the disadvantage of having to cover too wide a range of hand-types due to the lack of a clearcut takeout bid. Accordingly, responder is left guessing far too often.

Played alongside such as Lower Minor, it makes more sense as the double can always be a balanced hand and may occur more often than an out and

Terence Reese

Terence Reese was widely regarded as the greatest player writer of his generation. Many of his books are regarded as classics, notably *Reese on Play* and *The Expert Game*. He was a member of the British team that won the Bermuda Bowl in 1955, but ten years later in the same competition, he and Boris Schapiro were involved in the most famous accusation of cheating that the

game has ever known. Reese's book *Story of an Accusation* is a brilliant account of what happened.

He managed to get bridge onto the radio and wrote columns for many leading newspapers and periodicals. His 'over the shoulder' articles that appeared in *BRIDGE Magazine* were turned into a series of outstanding books. He collaborated with David Bird on many books, including the popular series about the Abbot.

out penalty double. It does, however, suffer from all the previously mentioned flaws of any method where the takeout bid is not double.

Optional Double is quite a common defence among club players where, unfortunately, it is open to some abuse as the doubler's hand-type can, in some partnerships, be guessed rather easily from the speed and tone of the double.

Reese

Also known as the Combination Method, the takeout bid is double in fourth seat and over three of a minor, but 3NT in second seat over three of a major.

This at least has the merit of not being very space consuming, but it removes one of the most important natural bids, 3NT over three of a major. Also, as with Foxu, there is the slightly illogical aspect that double is penalty in second seat but takeout in fourth. This means that the system allows a second in hand trump stack to catch the opposition from either side but a fourth hand stack from neither. In most defensive situations, it works best to play the same methods from both sides of the table; what cannot be picked up from one side may then be caught from the other.

Two-suited Takeouts

The two-suited takeout bid in standard methods is the immediate cuebid, e.g. 3♣ – 4♣. Traditionally, it showed a very powerful hand, at least 5-5 in any two unbid suits. The more modern idea would be that partner should assume the two majors where that is possible and choose between them while, if the opposition bid a major, the cuebid would show the unbid major plus an unspecified minor, until proven otherwise. So the cuebid still shows an unspecified two-suiter, and if it is not the expected combination it must still be a very strong hand, able to cope with partner's choosing the wrong suit. If, however, the right combination is held, particularly both majors over a three of a minor opening, the strength requirements can be relaxed somewhat. Over 3♣ or 3◊, cuebid with:

♠ A Q J 4 3
♡ A Q J 4 3
◊ 7 3
♣ 6

You are not strong enough to insist on game, nor for the traditional cuebid, but the modern philosophy is that it is better to make the bid which will get you to the correct trump suit and risk being too high, rather than make an alternative bid, double or overcall, which may get you to the right level but in the wrong suit.

If your actual suits were hearts and diamonds and the opening bid was 3♣, you might want an extra ace or king before considering the cuebid, the point being that you may often have to go to the five level.

Halsall
In Halsall, an overcall shows a two-suiter, short in the bid suit; e.g. 3♣ – 3♠ shows hearts and diamonds.

This enables the two suits to be distinguished immediately, but the loss of the natural single-suited overcall is far too high a price to pay for that relatively small benefit.

Four-of-a-minor Two-suiter Takeouts
A relatively modern idea is that an overcall of four of a minor over three of a major should show a two-suiter with the bid minor plus the other major. Double is for takeout. These two-suiters can be a problem under normal methods, particularly when of only moderate strength, and when you hold one you will be very glad to be playing this method. Against that, you lose the natural single-suited overcalls of 4♣ and 4◊. I suspect that it is quite a close call whether the price is too high or not.

Though it would be nice to be able to bid four of a minor in a natural sense, experts try to avoid doing so when there is a reasonable alternative so feel that its frequency is quite low. You would be surprised at some of the hands with which the experts are willing to gamble on a 3NT overcall, because of its big pay-off when it succeeds, rather than a 'nothing' 4♣ or 4◊ bid.

DEFENCES TO HIGHER OPENINGS

Ripstra over a 3NT Opening

When a 3NT opening shows a long minor, whether solid or just a four-level pre-empt, an overcall of four of a minor is for takeout, showing shortage in the other minor. Double is strong and fairly balanced.

Four of a Suit

Best is to continue to play takeout doubles, just as at a lower level. Responder who has a balanced hand and doesn't really fancy his chances of making anything, should be more inclined to just pass the double and hope to get a plus score that way. In particular, responder to a takeout double of 4♠ should not go to the five level except to bid a contract he hopes to make. A sequence like:

West	North	East	South
4♠	Dble	Pass	4NT

should show at least two places to play. The doubler will normally bid his preferred minor but if, for example, he bids 5♣ and partner bids 5◇, he should realise that 4NT was based on the two red suits.

The fact that responder will only bid a contract he expects to make, means he will have a distributional hand to pull the double, otherwise he will just settle for a penalty. This means that, though the double is for takeout, it can also be made on a strong balanced hand to increase the penalty. The only hand-type which cannot double is one with a trump stack and insufficient values/support to be happy if partner removes it.

A 4NT overcall of a 4♡/♠ opening shows both minors, while a cuebid shows a strong two-suiter – usually not both minors.

ARTIFICIAL PRE-EMPTS

A good general rule is that if you come up against an unusual opening bid and have not discussed your defence:

(i) If the opening bid promises some length in the bid suit then double is for takeout; e.g. a Lucas Two.

(ii) If the opening bid promises length in some other suit, then double is strong balanced and a bid of the promised suit is for takeout; e.g a Transfer Pre-empt.

(iii) If no specific suit is guaranteed but the bid is normally forcing, double is strong balanced while pass then double is takeout; e.g 2NT showing Any Weak Pre-empt.

2♠/NT = A Pre-empt in an Unspecified Minor

In second seat, double shows a reasonable balanced hand, double then double again is for penalties. When available, 2NT is natural but based on a long suit as a source of tricks rather than a defensive hand. 3♣/◇ is a non-forcing takeout bid showing shortage in the other minor.

In fourth seat, double is for takeout but will also have to be made on strong balanced hands. Overcalls are natural.

2NT = A Weak Minor Two-suiter

In second seat, double shows a good balanced hand and 3♣/◇ are both for takeout. There are two versions: 3♣ shows better hearts than spades, 3◇ shows better spades; 3◇ is stronger than 3♣. My preference is for the latter, but I doubt that there is much in it.

In fourth seat, over 3♣ double is strong balanced and 3◇ for takeout; over 3◇, double is for takeout but may include strong balanced hands.

3♣ = A Weak Minor Two-suiter

In fourth seat, as above; in second seat, double is strong balanced and double is for takeout.

Transfer Pre-empts

Where a pre-empt shows the suit above that opened (e.g. 3◇ shows hearts), in second seat, a bid of the suit shown is for takeout, double is strong balanced, and pass then double is for penalties. In fourth seat, assuming that the transfer was completed, double is for takeout.

Part 5
General Competitive Bidding

Lebensohl

When partner opens 1NT and the next hand intervenes, this can create an awkward problem.

For example, if the 1NT opening was weak, 12-14, and the next hand overcalled 2♠, you might wish to bid your long suit with each of these hands:

(i) ♠ 7 3   (ii) ♠ A 3
     ♡ K J 7 6 4 3   ♡ K J 7 6 4
     ◇ K 8   ◇ K 8 3
     ♣ 10 9 3   ♣ K 10 9

In the first case you would like to bid 3♡ purely as a competitive action, while with hand (ii) you want to make the same bid as a force, to help to decide whether to play 4♡ or 3NT.

Of course, playing standard methods you cannot do both.

This is where Lebensohl comes in. The idea is very simple; an immediate bid of 3♣ / ◇ / ♡ is natural and forcing; with the competitive hand you bid 2NT, which is artificial and commands partner to bid 3♣. Now you pass with clubs or bid 3◇ / ♡ as a competitive bid which partner is expected to pass.

So hand (i) qualifies for 2NT followed by 3♡ and hand (ii) is an immediate 3♡ bid.

There is a little more to Lebensohl than that, but the above was the main reason for its invention. The price you pay is the loss of the natural 2NT bid, but you get another benefit to help to more than compensate for that. The artificial 2NT bid means that you have no less than four game-forcing auctions available on balanced hands: an immediate 3NT or cuebid, and 2NT followed by 3NT or a cuebid.

This allows you to differentiate between hands with and without four cards in the unbid major and between hands with and without a stopper in the opponents' suit. A full scheme over a 2♡ overcall might be as follows:

1NT – 2♡ – 2♠ = Competitive with spades
        2NT = Demands 3♣
        3◇   = Forcing with diamonds
        3♡   = Game-force, balanced with four spades and
               a heart stopper
        3♠   = Forcing with spades
        3NT = To play, heart stopper but not four spades

After 2NT and the obligatory 3♣ reply, Pass shows clubs and 3◇ is to play; 3♡ shows four spades but no heart stopper and 3NT shows neither four spades nor a heart stopper; 3♠ is invitational with spades. It is assumed that all suit bids show five plus cards, immediate or via 2NT. It is now up to opener to decide on the best game contract.

The version above is something called Fast Arrival Shows Stopper (**FASS**), i.e. an immediate 3NT or cuebid shows a stop in the enemy suit, a delayed bid denies one. Some change things around and play that an immediate 3NT or cuebid denies a stopper, the delayed bid shows. This is Fast Arrival Denies Stopper (**FADS**). There is some very marginal technical benefit to the latter version but it is more than outweighed in my view by memory problems – a jump to 3NT sounds natural, doesn't it, so why not play it that way, showing a stopper?

There is one more important decision to make and that is the meaning of double. Traditionally, double of an overcall was for penalties. Takeout doubles are in these days in all sorts of situations including this one. A third possibility is for double to be optional, showing at least a raise to 2NT and letting partner decide.

The last style solves the problem of the lost natural 2NT bid, but is sometimes awkward to respond to. Penalty doubles are easiest to handle but leave many awkward hands. Takeout doubles make competition easiest of the three styles, but miss penalties and, if opener is ever to convert them for penalties, some discipline and partnership understanding is needed; it is, for example, dangerous to make a takeout double when void in the suit bid.

You can find people who will swear that one of the above styles is the only right one – supporters of each – but it is very close really. Whichever approach you choose, you will often wish you had chosen differently. I have a very marginal preference for takeout doubles, but it really is marginal.

Whatever you choose will be correct for you because you will choose what suits your general feeling about competitive bidding.

Lebensohl was originally created to cope with the problems when an opponent comes in over our 1NT, but it, or some modification of the same principle, can be used in many other competitive situations.

Transfer Lebensohl

If transfers are a good idea opposite a 1NT opening, why abandon them just because an opponent overcalls? There is no room to play them at the two level now but, assuming a two-level overcall, they can certainly be played at the three level, overcoming one of the problems with standard Lebensohl, namely that if the fourth hand raises you sometimes never get to show which suit you hold in a competitive hand. Transfer Lebensohl works like this:

1NT − 2♠ − 2NT = Clubs
           3♣ = Diamonds
           3◇ = Hearts, competitive or GF
           3♡ = Natural and invitational
           3♠ = Cuebid
           3NT = To play

1NT − 2♡ − 2♠ = Competitive
           2NT = Clubs
           3♣ = Diamonds
           3◇ = Transfer cuebid
           3♡ = Spades, at least invitational
           3♠ = Natural, forcing with a heart stop
           3NT = To play

Where a bid is a transfer to a long suit, opener is supposed to simply complete the transfer. With a competitive hand, responder passes; if he bids on, he has a game force. This means that the suit is always known immediately, allowing opener to compete with a fit if necessary. With a game-going hand, responder can bid a second suit, repeat the first one, or bid 3NT or cuebid as appropriate.

The idea of the transfer cuebid will be new to most readers. It shows a game-going balanced hand. To get over the problems of showing and denying stoppers in the opponents' suit, the scheme is that with no stopper opener simply completes the transfer, leaving partner in charge. With a stopper, opener makes a descriptive bid, either bids a four-card major or 3NT.

Where a bid is described as at least invitational, opener completes the transfer with a minimum but makes a descriptive bid with a maximum.

As with the original Lebensohl, you have to decide on the meaning of double.

It will come as no surprise that there are other versions of this in use but I am convinced that they are all a step forward on ordinary Lebensohl. What Lebensohl has is wide application in different situations. Transfer Lebensohl is only really appropriate where the main problem is to differentiate between forcing and competitive hand-types, i.e. you are always bidding by choice. Situations where you are sometimes bidding only because partner has forced you to do so, such as opposite a takeout double, are more suitable for Lebensohl.

Balancing in Fourth Seat

Generally, overcalls and doubles can be lighter than in second seat. In particular, a protective takeout double may be made on about an ace or king less than would be required in second seat. It follows that strength showing responses (anything other than a simple bid in a new suit) need to be correspondingly stronger. The theory is that the doubler continues to bid as though a king stronger than is actually the case, while responder bids as though a king weaker, all the way to the end of the auction.

1NT

While a second seat overcall of 1NT is always strong, it is normal to play it as weaker in fourth seat. The protective no-trump is played with many different ranges – as low as 10-12 for some pairs. To fit all the possible ranges on which you might want to bid into a sensible scheme, something like 11-15 is probably best. This allows double followed by 1/2NT to show 16-18 and an immediate 2NT to show 19-21.

If 1NT is to have such a wide range, you will probably need an enquiry bid opposite it. A very simple scheme, which could certainly be improved upon with a little effort is as follows:

Play all your responses exactly as if facing an opening bid of 1NT with the exception of 2♣. Here, this should be a combination of Stayman and range enquiry. Play that in response a minimum hand bids as if opposite normal Stayman, i.e. at the two level; a maximum makes the same response but at the three level; a middle range hand bids 2NT and now responder can bid 3♣ to check for a four-card major.

The advantage of the above is that it gets the job done reasonably well without adding much to the system and therefore the memory strain remains at a low level.

2NT

Whatever 2NT is in second position, it should be natural in fourth, somewhere around 19-21 HCP. If it is treated as two-suited, you make it very difficult to fit in all the strong balanced hand-types.

Responses, as always, should be as to an opening 2NT bid.

The Jump Overcall

Again, whatever you play in second seat, protective jump overcalls should be intermediate, i.e. a good six-card suit and sound opening values. It makes little sense to play weak jumps here, after all, if nothing else appeals you can just pass with a weak hand. Meanwhile, intermediate jumps help to take the strain off the simple overcall and describe your hand-type well in one bid.

The Cuebid

It is possible to play the cuebid just as in second seat, but given that you have already lost one part of your two-suited overcalling structure, it may be better to play that the fourth seat cuebid shows an unspecified goodish two-suiter – the kind of hand where you would be a little uncomfortable making a simple overcall but which is unsuitable for a takeout double (like most two-suiters).

If you adopt that style, responses in a new suit will be for correction, i.e. only to play if you have hit one of the cuebidder's suits, and 2NT would be a forcing enquiry.

Doubles

Competitive Doubles

A Competitive Double is a takeout double which applies in auctions where your side has overcalled but not yet found a fit. Take these two sequences:

(a) 1◇ – 1♠ – 2◇ – Dble
(b) 1◇ – 1♠ – 2♣ – Dble

In each case, you are pretty unlikely to wish to make a penalty double.

In (a), a Competitive Double would suggest either the other two suits or at least the ability to play in more than one denomination and sufficient strength to be able to cope with unwelcome developments in the auction.

In (b), the double usually suggests the unbid suit (in this case hearts) plus some support for partner's suit (spades).

Precise lengths or strengths promised are a matter for agreement, but the basic idea makes sense as otherwise the double will rarely be used.

Game Try Doubles

A Game Try Double occurs in a competitive sequence where the order of the suits means that there is no room to make a game try in any other way. The classical example is the following sequence:

West	North	East	South
1♠	2♡	2♠	3♡
?			

Sometimes, West will wish to bid 3♠ here purely to compete and will not wish to hear partner going on to game. On other occasions, West will want to bid 3♠ as a game invitation. Clearly, there is no legal way to achieve both of these goals.

The solution is to play a double as inviting game, nothing to do with penalties, and 3♠ as purely competitive. It is as simple as that. It will be rare for partner to convert the double for penalties because West could double on a wide range of different shapes and high card strengths.

It is possible to play double as a game try whichever two suits are involved, but it is only necessary where the opener's suit is immediately above that of the opposition, as above. In the above sequence, if North/South were bidding diamonds, 3♡ could be used to invite game, though saying nothing about hearts, and 3♠ competitive. Given that both sides have found a fit, double should not be out and out penalty but perhaps show a strong balanced hand, allowing partner to pass or go back to 3♠ as seems appropriate.

There are other situations in which Game Try Doubles could be used but none are as clearly right as this one.

Lead-directing Doubles of 3NT

A double of an opposing bid of 3NT is usually lead-directing, though it may be clear that you are merely suggesting that the cards are lying so badly for declarer that the contract will go down if partner simply makes his normal lead. Where it is lead-directing, it will ask for a different lead according to how the auction has gone.

If the opposition have bid 1NT – 3NT, a double is usually played as asking partner to lead his weaker major, the assumption being that the doubler has a running or near-running suit and the weaker major is most likely to be it. Some pairs prefer to specify a suit, saying that the double always asks for, say, a spade lead. With solid hearts, you just Pass and hope partner finds the lead. The main thing is to have some arrangement.

Where the declarer's side has had a free auction but has bid a number of suits along the way, a double traditionally asked for a lead of dummy's first bid suit. Where that suit has been bid and rebid strongly, so that it is inconceivable that partner can want it led, the most likely explanation is that he has at least one stopper in it and thinks some other obvious choice should succeed. Often, this will be a second suit bid by dummy.

Where the defenders have been in the bidding, a double usually suggests that partner lead his own suit. The theory is that, particularly when both defenders have bid a suit, the opening leader will tend to lead his partner's suit rather than his own if left to himself. Accordingly, double is used to make him lead his own suit.

Where only the doubler has bid a suit, the traditional meaning of a double was to demand that this suit be led. There is an attractive

Ted Lightner

Theodore A 'Ted' Lightner was Life Master #7 when the category was created by the ACBL in 1936. He was a graduate of Yale and the Harvard Law School and had a seat on the New York Stock Exchange.

He played with Ely Culbertson during the famous Culbertson–Lenz challenge match, later helping him to develop his system, and was a member of the team that won a series of challenge matches against British teams in the early thirties. Those were the days when Bridge made the front page, and thousands queued to get into Selfridges to watch! Lightner won every major title in America, and became a World Champion in 1953, when the USA won the Bermuda Bowl. He was an outstanding theoretician, and he shared his ideas, including his most famous invention, the double that bears his name, through his articles that appeared in *The Bridge World*.

alternative. If you assume that partner will normally lead your suit anyway, there is no need to double merely to direct the lead (though you may still wish to do so to increase the penalty), so a double should be used to tell partner to try a surprise lead. Depending on the auction, this may be a lead of dummy's suit or, more likely, an unbid suit – the doubler may have a two-suiter. English Bridge Union regulations prevent the use of such a double in conjunction with a psychic bid (i.e. overcall a suit you do not have then double to get partner to lead your real suit).

Lightner Doubles

A Lightner Double is a double of a freely bid slam contract. The assumption is that you will rarely be in a position to double such a contract merely to increase the size of the penalty and that when you are certain of defeating the contract you will be happy with your result undoubled. Hence, it makes sense to use the double to increase your chance of defeating the contract at all. In other words, it should be lead-directing.

The one thing such a double will not ask for is the lead of a suit bid by the defending side. Instead, it asks for an unusual lead, sometimes a suit bid by dummy, sometimes a suit which the doubler hopes to be able to ruff, in which case it could be any side suit, bid or not. If partner makes a Lightner Double and you cannot see an obvious lead, try the suit in which you have the greatest length and which it is remotely possible on the auction that he might be void.

Negative (Sputnik) Doubles

Negative, or Sputnik as they were originally called, Doubles apply when partner opens the bidding and the next hand overcalls. A Negative Double is not for penalties but is for takeout, showing a desire to bid but no clearcut bid is available. The classic Negative Double would show 4-4 in the unbid suits and not enough support for partner to raise him. For example: 1♡ – 2♣ – ? Holding:

> ♠ A 8 7 5
> ♡ 7 6
> ◇ K J 8 4
> ♣ 10 3 2

a Negative Double is the ideal solution.

Strength requirements are merely sufficient strength to wish to compete at this level and an ability to cope with whatever response partner makes. At the one or two level this need only be 7/8 HCP upwards. While the basic Negative Double shows about 7-10 HCP and support for the unbid suits, it need not be limited to that.

There is no reason not to start with a double with a much stronger hand if you have no long suit to bid. After all, you can always double then cuebid on the next round to force to game and show your extra values.

It tends to be agreed that a Negative Double promises four cards in an unbid major and this certainly makes partner's life easier, but this need not be a rigid requirement if you are able to cope if partner 'supports' the major.

If a Negative Double is played as unlimited, it means that a general game force never needs to cuebid the opponents' suit. This is good news for two reasons. Firstly, such a cuebid wastes bidding space compared to doubling then cuebidding, if necessary, on the next round. Secondly, it means that the immediate cuebid can be reserved for a specific hand-type, namely a constructive raise of opener's suit. If you play 1♡ – 1♠ – 2♠ as a constructive raise to at least 3♡, you release 1♡ – 1♠ – 3♡ to be pre-emptive, a good competitive approach.

If playing these doubles, you obviously cannot make a penalty double as partner will read it as for takeout. With a penalty double you just Pass and wait for partner to reopen. It follows that opener is expected to reopen, even

Alvin Roth

Alvin Roth is considered by many to be the leading bidding theorist of his generation. He is credited with the development of many ideas, notably the Negative Double and the Unusual No-Trump. With Tobias Stone he invented The Roth-Stone System, which emphasised sound bids. It was said this was because poor results bothered him, and he couldn't afford to lose at rubber bridge! Roth used to give one-man panel shows at tournaments, claiming he could not speak for more than an hour unless he was asked lots of questions. At one such event, the first question was 'Why did we lose to the Italians?' and if no bridge had been scheduled Roth would probably still be talking!

Apart from an entire system, his contributions to bidding theory include the unusual notrump, weak two bids, the forcing notrump and negative doubles. When he represented America for the first time in a World Championship, Roth, playing in Two Spades, felt he had played the hand before. As all the boards were hand dealt, the director doubted his claim, but Roth was able to identify all the cards in the other three hands, down to the spots! No-one has any idea how it happened. Born in 1914, Roth is still going strong, educating today's players through his regular articles in *Bridge Today*.

with a minimum, unless he has sufficient length in the overcaller's suit to be confident that responder does not have the penalty-pass type of hand.

A regular partnership needs to agree what sort of hand might make a Negative Double then bid a new suit on the next round. Traditionally, this has shown a long suit with insufficient strength to bid freely on the first round. So: 1♡ – 2♣ – Dble – Pass – 2◇ / ♡ – Pass – 2♠ might be bid on:

$$\begin{array}{ll} \spadesuit & \text{Q J 10 9 6 3} \\ \heartsuit & 7 \\ \diamondsuit & \text{K 5 4} \\ \clubsuit & 9 7 3 \end{array}$$

I have never liked this style but it is quite popular so perhaps it is just my personal prejudice.

Negative Free Bids

If you play Negative Doubles, you also have the option of playing Negative Free Bids. All that means is that a sequence such as 1♡ – 2♣ – 2♠ becomes non-forcing, based on a five- or six-card suit, and that if you want to make a forcing bid in a new suit you have to start with a Negative Double and then bid your suit on the next round. So 1♡ – 2♣ – 2♠ would show up to 10 HCP, while 1♡ – 2♣ – Dble then bid spades next time shows 11+ and is a one round force. Hence, the example above:

♠ Q J 10 9 6 3
♡ 7
◇ K 5 4
♣ 9 7 3

would be able to bid an immediate 2♠, but:

♠ A Q 10 9 6
♡ 7 2
◇ K J 4
♣ K 8 3

would have to start with a double then bid 2/3♠ on the next round.

Negative Free Bids can be quite effective when they come up, but do make constructive bidding more difficult when responder has a good hand, particularly if the fourth player can find a pre-emptive raise. They are probably best suited to systems where opener will frequently have a weak no-trump type when he opens one of a suit. For example, if playing a strong no-trump with five-card majors, you might play Negative Free Bids opposite a 1♣/◇ opening, which will be a weak no-trump type 40-50% of the time, but not opposite a 1♡/♠ opening.

Negative Slam Doubles

In a competitive auction where one side has bid a slam to make and the auction and vulnerability suggest that the other side might wish to consider a sacrifice, Negative Slam Doubles can be used to help to decide whether to sacrifice or not.

Over the slam bid, second hand doubles to show no defensive tricks but passes with one or more tricks.

If second hand doubles, then fourth hand passes with two or more defensive tricks but sacrifices with zero or one.

If second hand passes, fourth hand also passes with one or more tricks but doubles with no tricks. Now the second hand sacrifices if he has only one trick but passes with two or more.

Negative Slam Doubles are a good idea in auctions where a sacrifice is a live possibility. There are two problems. The first is to make sure that you are both on the same wavelength about what constitutes a possible sacrifice auction. A set of clearcut guidelines is advisable. The second is that it is not always clear how many defensive tricks your hand contains so a fair degree of judgement is required. But then you would need just the same judgement if you were not playing Negative Slam Doubles so only the possibility of a misunderstanding is really a new worry.

Responsive Doubles

A Responsive Double applies whenever partner makes a takeout double and the next hand raises his partner's suit. Now, by agreement, your double can also be for takeout, showing enough values to want to bid something but having no clearcut bid available. The simplest example is a sequence like: 1♡ – Dble – 2♡ – Dble, but others are possible including: 1♡ – 2♣ – Dble (negative) – 3♣ – Dble.

It is rare to want to make a penalty double when the opposition bid and raise a suit, particularly at a low level. Meanwhile, it is quite common to have the values to bid but no attractive choice. On the first auction, for example:

♠ K J 4
♡ 6 3
♢ K 8 7 4
♣ Q J 9 5

Why guess which suit to bid when you can make a Responsive Double and ask partner to choose?

There are two decisions to make. Thie first is to what level to play the double as responsive. Popular choices in the tournament world are 3♠ or 4♢, but anything is possible. The second decision is whether a Responsive Double denies anything about distribution.

For example, if you stick rigidly to the style where a takeout double of one major pretty well guarantees support for the other major, you may be happy to bid 1♡ – Dble – 2♡ – 2/3♠ on any four-card suit. If that is the case, you may decide that a Responsive Double should deny four cards in the unbid major. There is no right and wrong answer to this, but a regular partnership should know each other's style.

It is also possible to play that a double is responsive even when RHO changes the suit, for example: 1♡ – Dble – 2♣ – Dble. This is not standard and my own preference is to keep this double as penalty, but it is a perfectly reasonable style. With a stranger, it should be assumed that this type of double is not responsive unless specifically agreed.

Rosenkranz Doubles and Redoubles

Where partner overcalls and the third hand makes a positive call, a possible use of double and redouble is to show a top honour in partner's suit, particularly valuable if partner will be on lead against the final contract. The auctions: 1♡ – 1♠ – Dble (negative) – Rdbl, and 1♡ – 1♠ – 2♣ – Dble each show one of the top three spade honours if playing this way. It follows that a raise to 2♠ would show three card support but deny a top honour.

Support Doubles

In a competitive auction, it is often very important to be able to count the number of trumps held by your side in its suit as an aid to judging how far to compete. Support Doubles are a useful tool, normally used when third hand responds in a new suit and fourth hand makes a simple overcall. For example, after: 1◇ – Pass – 1♠ – 2♣ – ?, playing Support Doubles, any spade raise guarantees four-card support, while a double shows precisely three spades. The double says nothing about the strength of opener's hand; he may have a minimum opening or anything up to a hand where he intends eventually to drive to game. For the moment, he shows his three- card support by doubling and any other bid tends to deny three spades. With a good hand, of course, the doubler intends to bid on over partner's reply, making whatever seems the most appropriate descriptive bid.

If opener actually has a penalty double of the overcall he cannot make it. Instead he must either bid the appropriate number of no-trumps to describe his range or just pass and hope that partner can reopen with a takeout double which, of course, he will pass. At tournament level, many

George Rosenkranz

George Rosenkranz is equally well known as a famous scientist, the founding Chairman of the Syntex Corporation. He pioneered work on both cortisone and birth control pills. He has represented Mexico in world championship play almost continuously since 1962. In 1975 he created the 'Rosenkranz Award' presented annually by the International Bridge Press Association for the best bid hand of the year. Apart from his contributions to theory, he developed the Romex system.

pairs play these doubles as takeout anyway, so the loss of the penalty double is not so important.

Whether Support Doubles are a better idea than more general takeout doubles is unclear, depending on the basic system in use. Playing a weak no-trump four-card major system such as Acol, opener will frequently hold a strong no-trump type of hand which will be best described by a takeoutish double. Playing strong no-trump five-card majors and prepared minors, opener will often have a weak no-trump type. Now the Support Double becomes more important as you may often wish to compete with useful three-card support but this runs the risk of partner getting over excited. A Support Double acts as a useful compromise. Note also that opener is now less likely to hold a strong balanced hand after this start.

Responding to Takeout Doubles

2NT as a Scramble

It is rare in a competitive auction that 2NT is the exactly right contract. Many tournament pairs have therefore given up that option and play it in various artificial ways according to the precise situation. One popular use is as a scramble, showing two or more places to play opposite a takeout double. For example:

West	North	East	South
Pass	1♠	Pass	2♠
Pass	Pass	Dble	Pass
2NT			

There is no guarantee that East will have four-card support for any given suit so if West has two of them himself he would like to make sure that he does not guess wrongly. A 2NT scramble, promising at least two places to play is the solution.

Partner should normally choose his better minor here. If that proves to be one of West's suits he will pass, otherwise he will bid his cheapest suit.

The assumption here is that the doubler will always have at least two suits himself. In that case, a sensible fit can always be found. Suppose these are the two hands:

West	East
♠ 7 3 2	♠ J 2
♡ J 8 7 4	♡ Q 10 6 3
◇ A 9 6 3	◇ K J 2
♣ K 6	♣ A 9 7 3

Without the scramble, West would have to guess whether to bid 3♢ or 3♡. Playing the scramble he bids 2NT and East bids 3♣, his better minor. That doesn't suit West so he bids 3♢, showing diamonds and hearts, and now East can bid 3♡ – a much more comfortable contract than 3♢.

There are a number of competitive auctions in which the scramble can be useful, in particular, where game is unlikely and the main concern is to find the best partscore.

2NT as Lebensohl (Good/Bad 2NT)

A second use of 2NT in competitive situations is as a version of Lebensohl, usually called the Good/Bad 2NT by its users. Try this auction:

West	North	East	South
1♠	Dble	2♠	?

South may wish to bid a suit here on quite limited values, largely as a competitive move, but also on a much better hand with more constructive intent.

For example:

(i) ♠ 7 3 2
   ♡ K 8
   ♢ J 6 3
   ♣ Q 10 7 5 4

(ii) ♠ 7 3 2
   ♡ K 8
   ♢ J 6 3
   ♣ A Q 10 7 5

Hand (i) wants only to compete, while hand (ii) wants to encourage partner to bid on. If 2NT is Good/Bad (or Lebensohl), this becomes possible. A hand which merely wishes to compete bids 2NT, asking partner to bid 3♣, then passes or bids its suit next time; a more constructive hand bids its suit immediately.

In a sequence where you are obliged to bid, such as opposite a takeout double of a weak two bid, the distinction should be between weak and invitational; where you could have passed, as above, there are two ways of playing, either two different strengths of non-forcing bid, one competitive and the other invitational, or one competitive and the other forcing. I prefer the former, as hands which wish to force can usually cuebid or jump, not always ideal but rarely impossible.

Both Good/Bad and Scramble are useful ideas for regular partnerships. There are some situations where it is unclear which is the better meaning. Perhaps a good practical rule is to say that Scramble applies in all balancing auctions, where we have passed often enough to make it likely that we are just competing the partscore, while Good/Bad applies when we come into the auction earlier so that game is still a live possibility. That still leaves scope for some discussion as to what constitutes a balancing auction. Play both and you will eventually discover one where you and partner do not see eye to eye.

4NT as Two Places to Play

When no suit is agreed, even by inference, 4NT can hardly be Blackwood, especially if you play one of the more exotic types such as RKCB. A very good idea in certain high-level auctions is for a 4NT bid to be a kind of scramble, usually showing two places to play.

After 4♠ – Dble – Pass – ? you may not wish to defend, the double being essentially for takeout, but not know which suit to bid, say:

♠ 6
♡ A J 8 6
◇ J 9 3
♣ K 10 7 6 3

At this level, partner may be under pressure to double with some less than ideal distributions, so to bid 5♡ and then complain when he fails to provide four-card support would be foolish. Equally, he may have only two or three clubs. The solution is to bid 4NT, two places to play. Partner bids his lowest playable suit and, if it is clubs, you Pass. If it is diamonds, you bid 5♡, trusting him to have two suits for his takeout double. You may not always reach your best fit, but you greatly increase the chance of reaching a sensible one.

For those who want more for their money, you can add in two different ways to get to 5♡, allowing one to be to play and the other a definite slam invitation. Simply bid 5♡ immediately if willing to hear partner go on to slam, bid 4NT with the weaker variety and bid 5♡ whichever minor partner chooses. So though 4NT is basically a scramble, there is a small element of Good/Bad in there as well.

Defending Two-suited Overcalls

Unusual Over Unusual

Unusual over Unusual is a defence to two-suited overcalls, in particular the Unusual No Trump. It allows the opener's partner to make both competitive and constructive raises of opener's major suit and forcing and non-forcing bids in the other major. The simplest version is as follows:

1♠ – 2NT –   3♣ = Forcing with 5+ hearts
             3◇ = Good raise to 3♠ or more
             3♡ = Non-forcing with long hearts
             3♠ = Weaker spade raise

1♡ – 2NT – 3♣ = Good heart raise
            3◇ = Forcing with spades
            3♡ = Weaker heart raise
            3♠ = Non-forcing with spades

A less popular but sensible variation swaps round the meaning of 3◇ and 3♠ after a 1♡ opening, allowing an opener who hates spades to repeat his hearts over the weaker of the spade bids. He always has a chance opposite the forcing bid, of course.

Some methods are needed here and one or other version seems sensible. Double should be more penalty orientated, denying primary trump support for opener.

Defences to Other Two-suited Overcalls

Some systems of two-suited overcalls specify only one suit, for example a Michaels Cuebid of 1M – 2M. In this case, the cuebid should show a constructive raise in opener's suit and an immediate raise should be more pre-emptive. New suits are normally played as natural and forcing.

Other methods specify both suits immediately. Take a Ghestem cuebid such as 1♠ – 2♠, showing hearts and clubs. Where both cuebids are available below three of partner's suit, as here, best is to play that the higher cuebid, in this case 3♡, shows a constructive raise, while a raise would be pre-emptive. A bid in the fourth suit could now be natural but non-forcing and the lower cuebid show a forcing bid in the fourth suit; so in the current example 3♣ would be a forcing 3◇ bid and 3◇ natural but non-forcing.

For example:

	(i)		(ii)		(iii)	
	♠ A Q 5 3		♠ A 2		♠ 3 2	
	♡ K 6 2		♡ J 4		♡ J 4	
	◇ Q 10 5 3		◇ A Q 10 9 6 5		◇ A Q J 9 8 7	
	♣ 7 4		♣ K 3 2		♣ 7 3 2	

After partner opens 1♠ and the next hand overcalls 2♠, showing hearts and clubs, hand (i) bids 3♡, showing a constructive raise to at least 3♠; (ii) bids 3♣, a forcing bid in diamonds; (iii) bids 3◇, natural and non-forcing.

Beware of the assumption that this applies every time that both suits are specified. After a Ghestem 3♣ overcall, the meaning of the cuebid(s) may vary according to which suit was opened. E.G. 1♠ – 3♣, showing hearts and diamonds. You have no convenient club bid. Assuming double to be negative, best is to play 3♡ as the constructive spade raise and 3◇ as forcing with clubs. But after 1♡ – 3♣, showing spades and diamonds, there is only one cuebid below 3♡, best is for 3♢ to show a constructive heart raise. Maybe 3♠ should be forcing with clubs and 4♣ non-forcing, but you will rarely want a non-forcing natural 4♣ bid. The real message is that a serious partnership must discuss each sequence individually once they choose to go down this road at all.

Raising Partner In Competition

When we open the bidding with one of a suit and the opposition intervene, the auction is by definition a competitive one and the methods at our disposal should bear more relation to those used after we have overcalled than to those we use an uncontested auction.

Pre-emptive Raises

Just as opposite an overcall, an immediate jump raise should be more pre-emptive once the opposition intervene, whether with an overcall or a takeout double. Everyone is familiar with the notion that 1♡ – Dble – 3♡ is pre-emptive and 1♡ – Dble – 2NT shows a sound raise to 3♡. It makes sense for 1♡ – 1♠/2♣/♢ – 3♡ to show the same kind of pre-emptive hand. Vulnerability is a factor, but just how weak the pre-emptive raise can be is largely a matter of partnership style.

The Cuebid Raise

The reason why pre-emptive raises are possible in competition is that, just as opposite an overcall, if the opposition have bid a suit you must have a cuebid available. The simplest scheme is to play that a cuebid of the opponents' suit shows at least a limit raise to three of partner's suit. E.G. 1♡ – 1♠ – 2♠ shows a constructive raise to at least 3♡.

There is no other hand-type which needs to start with a cuebid, so the cost is almost zero.

2NT as a Raise

1♡ – Double – 2NT is a constructive heart raise. It is quite possible to play 1♡ – 1♠/2♣/♢ – 2NT the same way. With a natural 2NT bid you can always make a negative double then bid 2NT on the next round. Why should you want to do this, given that the cuebid is already available to show a constructive raise?

I can think of at least two possible reasons. Firstly, suppose that you play five-card major openings; you could play 2NT as a three-card raise and the cuebid as a four-card raise. In a world where everyone worships the Law of Total Tricks, counting trumps has become a way of life for many.

The other possibility is that you want to make pre-emptive raises on very weak hands and find that two ways of raising are simply not enough. I

discovered that I wanted to make three-level raises on all these hands after
1♡ – 1♠ – ?:

(a)	♠ 7 6 3	(b)	♠ 7 6 3	(c)	♠ 7 6 3
	♡ J 10 8 6		♡ K 10 8 6		♡ A Q 8 6
	◇ 5		◇ 5		◇ Q 8 5
	♣ 9 8 6 4 2		♣ K 9 8 6 4		♣ K 9 8

Hand (a) is a purely pre-emptive raise; hand (b) is low in high cards but is
worth an invitational raise because of the distribution (no, the clubs are
not good enough for a Fit-jump); hand (c) is worth an invitation based on
high card strength.

It would be no bad thing to be able to distinguish between hand-types (b)
and (c). It matters little which of 2NT and the cuebid shows which
hand-type, either way you will be helping partner's later judgement.

2NT can be used as an artificial raise opposite any suit when the
opposition have intervened with a takeout double, and also when we have
opened one of a major and they have overcalled. Where we have opened
one of a minor and they have overcalled, there is too much danger that we
will eventually want to play 3NT and playing it the right way up may be
crucial, so now 2NT should be natural.

Fit Jumps and Fit Non-jumps

Just as opposite an overcall, when we open the bidding and the auction
becomes competitive jump-shifts should be fit-showing. There is nothing
new to be said. For further details see the section on responding to
overcalls.